Yosemite
Trout Fishing Guide

Charles S. Beck

Frank
Amato
PORTLAND

Dedication

For our son Aaron, that we will spend many happy days together traveling to places of wild beauty in pursuit of wild trout.

Acknowledgments

Many fine people contributed to this book. I'd like to thank them all and express my sincere appreciation. To start, thanks to my parents Chuck and Jane Beck, for instilling in me at an early age an appreciation for places of natural beauty, for first taking me to Yosemite, and for buying me that first fishing rod. Thanks to my hiking and fishing companions Bill Beck, Matt Burtch, and Robert Olney, who made the miles on the trail even more enjoyable. Thanks to Linda Eade, Librarian, Yosemite National Park Research Library, for her cheerful assistance and to Michael Finley, Superintendent, Yosemite National Park, for his part in working for more catch and release fishing in Yosemite. Thanks to Rena and Rod Webster for their all-around helpfulness. Thanks to Jim Law and Bruce Fulmer for their stories of fishing the Merced River in years past. Thanks to Reverend Rod Craig for sharing his enthusiasm and appreciation for God's grand gift, Yosemite. Thanks to Dr. and Mrs. John M. Olney, Jr. for their constant support and their stories about the formation and early days of the Sierra Club. And finally, to my wife, thanks for all the miles you walked, all the pictures you took, all the pages you typed, all the fishing stories you had to listen to, all the waiting and worrying you endured while I wandered the backcountry, and all the nights you spent camping in the cold (with bears). Beth, this book would not have been possible without your love and encouragement.

Copyright 1995 by Charles S. Beck

ALL RIGHTS RESERVED. No part of this book may be reproduced without the written consent of the publisher, except in the case of brief excerpts in critical reviews and articles.

Published in 1995 by Frank Amato Publications, Inc.
P.O. Box 82112, Portland, Oregon 97282
ISBN: 1-57188-042-9
UPC: 0-66066-00238-9
Book Design: Charlie Clifford
Printed in Canada
1 3 5 7 9 10 8 6 4 2

Contents

Introduction

Yosemite National Park. Just saying, seeing, or hearing the name of this national treasure sets the mind into motion. Everyday concerns are instantly forgotten in favor of images of spectacular gushing waterfalls, majestic snow-capped peaks, and lush green meadows. Awesome views of the glacially carved granite landscape and stately giant sequoias flood the mind and intoxicate the soul.

As one who's fished extensively in Yosemite, I also see untamed cascading rivers, peaceful blue lakes, and babbling tree-lined creeks, as well as the beautiful wild trout that inhabit them.

In Yosemite there is water to be found that will suit every fisherman, from easily accessible roadside spots to remote, off-trail backcountry locations that require a week of strenuous hiking to reach. The 318 lakes and 1,361 miles of running water in the park (about half of which hold trout) are made up of tiny ponds, huge lakes, trickling creeks, and raging rivers. Fishermen will find the beauty of the surroundings unparalleled—whether fishing in Yosemite Valley, Tuolumne Meadows, or in the lakes and streams of the upper crest of the Sierra. The opportunity to catch wild trout in an area of awesome natural beauty is the enticing combination that has drawn me back to fish Yosemite time after time, year after year.

Yosemite is not often thought of as a fishing destination. For most visitors fishing is a mere sidelight to the scenery; a pleasant diversion to fill in the time between sightseeing excursions. This is no accident and I have no argument with this attitude. For the scenery is outstanding and the fishing is admittedly not in the same class as that of Yellowstone Park—which is as highly regarded for its fishing as it is for its beauty. The trout in Yosemite are generally smaller than those found in Yellowstone, but in many cases they are just as numerous. A good, well informed fisherman can still make fine catches in Yosemite, and looking down at a colorful rainbow in the net, then looking up at a 1,400 foot waterfall is the kind of experience that most people will remember always.

Today's Yosemite trout are all wild fish. Although fish stocking was carried out in Yosemite for over one hundred years, no stocking currently takes place. These wild, finely marked trout include the leaping, crimson-sided rainbow, the bold, gaudy brookie, the reclusive, defiant brown, and the isolated, highly prized state fish of California, the golden trout.

The information presented in this book covers, in exhaustive detail, the area in and around Yosemite National Park, including the trout wonderland that is the Eastern Sierra (where the trout fishing often does rival that of Yellowstone). The past ten years has seen me pulling on my backpack, lacing up my hiking boots, and heading for all parts of the park in pursuit of its wild trout. I've made hundreds of thousands of casts in these waters and have been fortunate enough to catch thousands of fish. The purpose of this book is not to draw a flood of fishing visitors to Yosemite, but rather to enhance the experience of those who venture to the park, by pointing out the little known angling opportunities that do exist. The trout fishing in Yosemite can be very good indeed if you know where and when to go, and what methods to use.

Vernal Falls and Merced River below. Photo by Rob Olney

General Information

The Trout of Yosemite

In Yosemite the rainbow is the only native trout. It and the introduced brook trout are by far the most populous fish in the park. Brown trout are the next most important trout from an angling standpoint, and are found in dozens of lakes and streams throughout Yosemite. The golden trout, California's beautiful state fish, is only encountered in a few waters—both lakes and creeks. The only other trout currently found, the cutthroat, is by far the rarest. This transplant remains only in one lake inside the park. Over the years there have been attempts at establishing other fish in Yosemite including lake trout, Dolly Varden, and grayling, but these have been unsuccessful.

Fishing Regulations

The fishing season for Yosemite is the same as for the rest of California. California's general stream trout season runs from the last Saturday in April until November 15. The Eastern Sierra waters are open the same times except in certain cases. Some waters on the east side close on October 31, two weeks earlier than the rest of the state. Closure dates change from year to year, so please check the current state regulations booklet before you fish.

The state limit on trout is five fish per day unless otherwise noted. Yosemite has adopted these regulations on all park waters except the Merced River in Yosemite Valley where all rainbow trout must be released. The Merced in Yosemite Valley is also the only place inside the park where there are gear restrictions. Only barbless hooks and artificial lures may be used—bait fishing in the valley is no longer allowed. The Eastern Sierra waters have many such restrictions. Again, these change, so be sure to consult the state fishing regulations to make sure you are fishing with a legal method.

Weather

The high country is usually snowed in until late May in a year of average snowfall. Low elevation waters (below 5,000 feet) are usually fishable when the trout season opens at the end of April. As a very general guide, the 5-6,000 foot elevation is usually free of ice and snow by early June, 6-7,000 feet by late June, 7-8,000 feet by early July, 8-9,000 feet by mid-July, and over 9,000 feet by late July. The high country usually provides good weather all through August and September. October can be clear (but cold) in the mountains, but can also see the first heavy snows of the winter season. These conditions do of course vary greatly from year to year. The middle of the summer usually sees clear sunny weather with some short periods of afternoon thundershowers. Daytime temperatures can get into the 80s even at high elevations, but nights can be cool even on the warmest days—

lows often dip into the 30s. Generally the weather in the Sierra is as good as is found in any mountain range in the world with sparkling sunny days being the rule rather than the exception. This is what prompted John Muir to call the Sierra Nevada the "Range of Light".

Maps

Good maps are a necessity when hiking in the mountains. The map handed out when entering Yosemite is a fine road map and general guide, but it won't do for hikers and backpackers. The best maps for the fisherman who wishes to leave the pavement are published by the U.S. Geological Survey. These topographic maps are available in varying degrees of detail, and are comprehensive in their coverage of the area described in this book. I've found that the 15 minute series is the best compromise between detail and convenience. The U.S.G.S. 15 minute topographic maps that apply to Yosemite and its immediate surroundings are: Pinecrest, Tower Peak, Matterhorn Peak, Bodie, Lake Eleanor, Hetch Hetchy, Tuolumne Meadows, Mono Craters, El Portal, Yosemite, Merced Peak, and Devils Postpile.

The Wilderness Press also publishes maps that cover the most popular parts of Yosemite. These maps are topographic maps of the 15 minute scale. The advantage of the Wilderness Press maps is that they are more up-to-date, (therefore more accurate), and more durable (waterproof and tearproof). The disadvantage is that they are a bit more expensive, and aren't currently available for all sections of Yosemite. They have 15 minute maps published of Hetch Hetchy, Tuolumne Meadows, Yosemite, Merced Peak, and Devils Postpile. The best overall map of the entire region is also a Wilderness Press work called "Yosemite National Park and Vicinity." This map can be purchased separately, and also accompanies the fine hiking guide they publish titled *Yosemite National Park* by Jeffrey Schaffer.

You can get some of these maps at area sporting goods stores, ranger stations, and Yosemite Visitor Centers. They can also be purchased by mail at the following addresses:

Wilderness Press
2440 Bancroft Way
Berkeley, CA 94704

U.S. Geological Survey
Building 41
Box 25286 Federal Center
Denver, C0 80225

Yosemite National Park Statistics
- Became a national park in 1890
- 758,123 acres
- about 800 miles of trails
- about 200 miles of roads
- 1,361 miles of rivers and creeks (approximately 40% of these contain trout)
- 318 lakes (approximately 40% of these also contain trout)

Best Trout Flies

Following are my choices for the flies I wouldn't want to be without when fishing Yosemite. If a bear got all my food and I had to hike three days to resupply, I'd feel confident about enjoying trout dinners if I had these flies.

Dry Flies

Adams #16—Probably the best all-around fly ever tied on a hook. Its colors match countless small mayflies and caddisflies.

Elk Hair Caddis #14—Caddisflies are the most commonly found large aquatic insect in Yosemite waters. The Elk Hair Caddis is a good imitation that floats well and is highly visible for the angler.

Black Ant #18—Trout love to eat ants, they are found near most lakes and streams, and many find their way into the water. A small ant pattern also can pass for the commonly found small black beetle, as well as for black midges.

Yellow Humpy #12—A great attractor pattern that floats well even in heavy currents. It mimics grasshoppers, large caddisflies, and large stoneflies on broken surfaces.

Wet Flies, Nymphs and Streamers

Gold Ribbed Hare's Ear #12—Probably the best all-around nymph ever tied on a hook. Its size, shape, and color imitates the majority of mayfly nymphs, stonefly nymphs, and caddis pupae that inhabit trout waters.

Pheasant Tail Nymph #18—A great nymph to use when trout are feeding on tiny subsurface fare. Small mayfly nymphs make up a large part of the diet of Sierra trout, and the P.T. Nymph is a dead ringer for these nymphs.

Woolly Worm #8—This versatile fly can be fished as a streamer to imitate minnows, or dead drifted to imitate large stonefly nymphs. Its long soft hackle also acts as a good attractor for wilderness trout that aren't too choosy.

Sparkle Caddis Pupae #14—During the many heavy caddis hatches encountered by mountain trout fishermen, a dry caddis pattern sometimes is ineffective when trout are seen leaping clear of the water. This is the time for a Sparkle Caddis fished below the surface. It can lead to some fast action in periods of caddis emergence.

Yosemite
National
Park

California

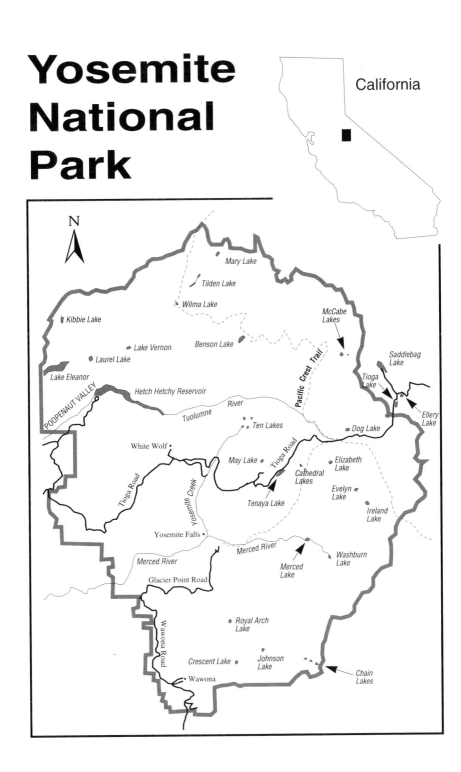

N

Mary Lake

Tilden Lake

Wilma Lake

McCabe Lakes

Kibbie Lake

Lake Vernon

Benson Lake

Saddlebag Lake

Laurel Lake

Tioga Lake

Lake Eleanor

POOPENAUT VALLEY

Hetch Hetchy Reservoir

Pacific Crest Trail

Ellery Lake

Tuolumne River

Ten Lakes

Dog Lake

White Wolf

May Lake

Tioga Road

Elizabeth Lake

Cathedral Lakes

Evelyn Lake

Tenaya Lake

Ireland Lake

Tioga Road

Yosemite Creek

Yosemite Falls

Merced River

Washburn Lake

Merced River

Merced Lake

Glacier Point Road

Wawona Road

Royal Arch Lake

Crescent Lake

Johnson Lake

Chain Lakes

Wawona

Merced River

Early Spanish explorers named it Rio de la Merced—The River of Mercy. The Merced River is the centerpiece of Yosemite National Park. It is the Merced that flows through the incomparable, world-renowned Yosemite Valley. The Merced leaps over two of the park's most spectacular waterfalls—Vernal Fall and Nevada Fall. This is the river seen by the most visitors to Yosemite and fished by the most anglers.

The river holds a surprisingly good population of trout despite the rather heavy fishing pressure it's received over the years. The main reason for this is the fact that although the Merced runs for over 30 miles inside the park, only a few miles of river (in Yosemite Valley) draw the bulk of fishermen. There is good fishing to be found the entire length of the river inside the park, as well as in the downstream portion on the western approach to the park. Much variety is encountered when fishing the Merced. All water types are found, from slow pools to rapids, and everything in between. The river's headwaters are at the 11,000 foot level, and when it leaves the park the elevation is about 2,000 feet.

The only native trout to the river is the rainbow. The upstream limit of these native fish was 317-foot Vernal Fall, which is located a couple of miles above Yosemite Valley. Rainbows have been planted above the falls, and can now be found in the entire length of the river. There have also been plantings of brown and brook trout, which continue to thrive in parts of the river.

The Indians that lived in Yosemite Valley, the Ahwahnechee, found the river to harbor a large population of rainbow trout. The trout were harvested by the tribe and made up a normal part of their diet. Once Yosemite became a popular tourist destination (in the late 1800s) some enterprising Indians began providing trout for the hotels in Yosemite Valley at a cost of 25 cents per pound. They first used straight hooks made of bone and line made of milkweed. Later, they obtained steel hooks from the tourists. Their usual bait was worms when fishing in the large Merced River.

In small creeks they sometimes used poisonous plants to stun the fish. Usually soaproot was used for this purpose. A small pool was selected and its escape routes were sealed with rocks. The plant was then submerged at the head of the pool so that the current would carry the poison throughout the water in the pool. This mild poison would stun the fish enough that they could be easily captured by hand. This method was only possible in small creeks during the low water season.

In the main Merced trout were of good size and good numbers in Yosemite Valley. An 1872 photo shows a Native American fisherman,

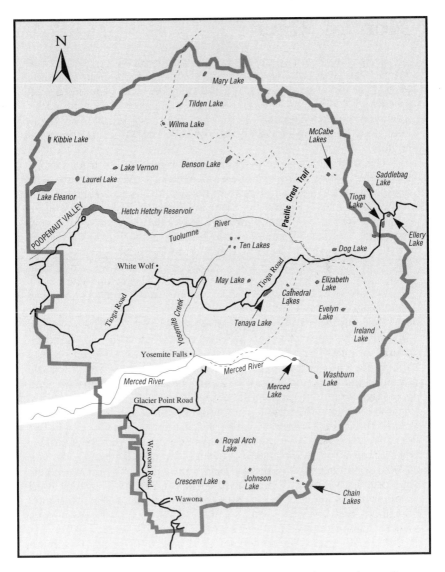

Indian Tom, with a nice stringer of 10-15 inch rainbows. The earliest accounts of trout fishing in Yosemite are found in James Hutching's book *In the Heart of the Sierras* published in 1886. Hutchings ran one of the first hotels in Yosemite Valley. He describes visitors attempting to catch the 'speckled mountain trout', as the rainbows were called, in the Merced River. The most successful method seemed to be fishing at night and using pieces of previously caught suckers for bait. One humorous account describes the single tiny trout a fancy city tourist

R. Noall standing by the Merced River with a 5 pound 14 ounce brown near the base of El Capitan. June 5, 1932.

took with his elaborate fly rod, while an Indian strolled in with a heavy stringer of fish caught with worms and a hand line.

The earliest of the sport fishermen fished the river in the 1870s, and this is the era when fish planting began. The first trout plant in the Merced River in Yosemite Valley was in 1879. The fishless areas above the waterfalls were planted in the early 1900s with brooks and rainbows. At the same time browns and cutthroats were planted in the Merced in the valley. There were also one time plants of Dolly Varden trout (at an unknown date) and grayling (in 1931). These were both planted in Yosemite Valley, and were both unsuccessful. The cutthroat plantings, of which there were four, were also unsuccessful. Today you won't find cutthroat, Dolly Varden, or grayling in the Merced River. The planting of brown trout in Yosemite was halted in 1948, but the biggest fish in the river continue to be browns. The biggest rainbows in the river are generally not caught in the park, but instead in the lower reaches of the river outside the park. In analyzing the different stretches of river I'll start with the lower river and work upstream into the park.

The lower Merced River lies in the great Central Valley below McSwain and McClure Reservoirs. There is some good but spotty trout fishing found in the lower river, but for our purposes we'll concentrate on the upper Merced above the reservoirs. Highway 140 joins the river at Briceburg and follows its course all the way to the head of Yosemite Valley. A good dirt road leaves Briceburg (which isn't a town as much as just a name on the map) and follows the river downstream for a few miles. This is a scenic and uncrowded place to fish (except for a few gold miners) and features many large deep pools connected by fast rapids and deep runs. There are some good rainbows in this section, but their numbers are small. The trout share this water with bass, and the bass fishing is better than the trout fishing here. The best fish are deep in the pools and runs, so bait fishermen generally have more success than fly fishermen.

As you move upstream from Briceburg back on the highway, the river has similar characteristics all the way up to the confluence with the South Fork. But, being right on the highway, its deep pools attract many summer fishermen (as well as many swimmers). This section still holds bass and some good-sized trout. Locals fish here in the spring and fall for two reasons. The first is to avoid the summer crowds, the second is that the fishing is better. The water gets too warm in summer, which slows down the activity level of the fish—they get more active when it cools off in fall. The river was previously open all year, but current regulations (which took effect in 1990) call for a closure from mid-November to the end of April.

In years when fishing is allowed all year, early spring can be a fine time to be on this stretch of river. Runoff hasn't yet begun in earnest so the river is still wadable. This is when the large stoneflies (salmonflies) can be found hatching. The hatch usually starts in this part of the river in mid-March, and moves upstream reaching the park by the first of May. The water is usually low and clear enough to fish in March, but spring runoff in mid-April makes fishing difficult when the hatch moves upstream. These giant insects are about two inches long and really excite the trout. Giant stonefly nymphs and dry flies in sizes four and six work well at imitating the natural. Bait fishermen who use the stoneflies they capture will greatly outfish their salmon egg and worm dunking counterparts during the hatch. The amount of insects hatching varies from year to year. Some years there are only a handful seen fluttering about, while other years they'll be found swarming all around the river. There are currently no regulations on this part of the river regarding fishing methods, and five fish per day may be kept.

Moving further upstream from the South Fork to the Red Bud Picnic Area the river changes slightly. The pools become smaller and less frequent, giving way to more riffles and pocket water. From here upstream to Yosemite Valley the Merced is a classic trout river. In fact, Charlie Brooks called it "the most typical of all the mountain trout streams I know" in his fine book, *Larger Trout for the Western Fly Fisherman*. This section is more suitable for fly fishing than the downstream section. It is shallower, easier to wade, has more insect life, and has an increased trout population. You'll still find some bass here— generally pan-sized smallmouths. The average trout may be a little smaller than you find downstream, but there are a lot more of them.

The best flies to use are giant stoneflies in the spring and caddisflies in summer and fall. A small olive-green caddis is found throughout the entire length of the river. They hatch in late afternoon and are found fluttering over the water's surface at dusk. The best sized flies to match the naturals are 14 and 16. Olive caddis pupa patterns and Zug Bug's work well all day. Sometimes letting the fly dead drift with the current is successful, while at other times it is better to strip the fly in giving it some life-like action. When adult flies are on the water an olive Elk Hair Caddis or Goddard Caddis will usually produce. Stonefly nymphs also work well in the riffles all summer long. In the colder months there can also be large *Baetis* mayfly hatches. A small (size 18-20) Blue Winged Olive or Adams matches this fly well. I took a pretty rainbow of about a pound-and-a-half here in December a couple of years ago on a size 18 Blue Winged Olive during one such hatch. The only other fish I caught that day was also on a dry fly during the *Baetis* hatch—a fine foot-long rainbow.

The part of this stretch to avoid when looking for wild fish is near Indian Flat Campground, where the river gets hit hard by fishermen. It is planted by the D.F.G. here, and few hatchery fish survive the fishing pressure. This stretch of river does hold a few big fish as long-time area fisherman Bruce Fulmer can attest. He's caught rainbows in the five to six pound range in these pools. However, since 1980 the big fish are getting more scarce, and a two pounder is considered a fine catch today.

From the Foresta Bridge at Red Bud Picnic Area upstream to the boundary of the National Park there are some restrictions in effect. This four mile section is open all year, but can only be fished with artificial lures possessing barbless hooks. Carry needle nosed pliers and pinch down your barbs before fishing here. The minimum size limit is 12 inches and only two trout may be kept. These regulations have been in effect since 1987, but I haven't noticed a dramatic improvement in the fishing. The main reason is most likely the extended drought that has gripped the Merced River drainage for the entire duration of the new regulations. With more water volume we probably will see the fish population get healthier. At the low levels the river has seen for the past five years the water gets much warmer than is ideal in the summer. More water volume also would mean more and better holding areas for the trout. It is currently very rare to catch, or even see, a trout over 15 inches in this section. There is a pretty good population of trout in the 8-12 inch range. Most of these are rainbows with some browns mixed in, although the browns will be bigger. In fact all the trout I've taken here over 13 inches have been browns. These four miles are ideal rainbow water for the fly fisherman. There are very few pools or slow spots. Most of it is pocket water, riffles, and rapids. Kayakers like this area during the spring runoff, but they won't get in your way because the river is usually very high and difficult to fish from April to June in a normal year.

The salmonfly hatch is sometimes fishable here, but most often it is only possible to fish the edges because of high water. It's hard to get around and cover much water at this time. Fly casting can be difficult on the brushy banks—which is the best place to float a salmonfly. The fish will be near the edges waiting for adult salmonflies to fall in the water. These big flies are spotted by trout even in water too cloudy for a fisherman to see the bottom of a shallow spot in the river. The fish aren't monsters, but the savage rises these 10-12 inch fish make to dry salmonflies bring me out to the river a couple of times every April.

In summer the water is wadable and clear—very clear. The trout aren't overly selective regarding the fly pattern if it is of the general size of the naturals. But, due to the extreme water clarity, I've found leader length and tippet size to be of the utmost importance. Many times I've been fishing along with only spotty success until I make the change to a lighter tippet. The fishing then improves two or three fold almost instantly. In anything but the fastest water, tippets shouldn't be larger than 5X. Spin fishermen should use no more than four pound test line; two pound test is ideal. The trout aren't so big that they can't be handled even on smaller tippet. I usually use 6X during the low water in the fall, and 7X when fishing the quiet pools. A seven 1/2 foot leader is fine for the fast water, but 10 feet or longer is recommended for the pools. This holds true for the entire river during late summer and fall. The same flies that are used downstream are effective up here in the summer. There are lots of tan and olive caddisflies in sizes 12-18. Giant stonefly nymphs are present year-round, and can be bounced along the bottom with good results. Nymphing is generally the most effective method for fishing during the day in summer on this water. Weighted size 14 Hare's Ears or size six Stonefly Nymphs work well in the pockets and riffles.

Despite being right next to a highway and being adjacent to a national park, this area still doesn't get an undue amount of fishing pressure. In the very early days before the highway was built, the few people fishing the river enjoyed some great sport. Jim Law, an El Portal resident since 1907, was one of these rare early fishermen. His father came to El Portal (just outside the western entrance to the park on the Merced River) to work on the Yosemite Valley Railroad. His grandfather had been a professional fly tier in Scotland, so young Jim naturally was drawn to fly fishing the river. He recalls taking many fine rainbows in those days, the biggest of which measured 23 inches and weighed seven pounds. That fish was caught right across from where the town's gas station now sits—about a mile outside the park.

From the park boundary up to Yosemite Valley the Merced River gets even less fishing pressure. Here the river flows down a rugged gorge. It's close to the road, but can still be a steep and sometimes dangerous climb to reach. There are some nice holes and pockets in the gorge, but the biggest problem is covering the water. I usually spend just as much time rock climbing as I do fishing down there. It's tough going even for those in good shape. Although you are never far from the road, it can seem at times like you're on a wilderness river. The sound of the current drowns out the passing vehicles and the trees obstruct the view of them. It's just you and the trout (there are plenty), and the rattlesnakes (there are a few), and the bears (I've only seen one here). The fishing can be surprisingly good because some of the less accessible areas probably see less than a dozen fishermen a year. I've fished it numerous times and have never seen another fisherman. The trout are about half browns and half rainbows, but you'll generally catch 75 percent rainbows. The gorge is the upper reach of the salmonfly hatch, but it usually isn't possible to fish because of the high water. In fact it can be difficult to fish here until late July because of high water—even in a normal water volume year.

In the summer grasshoppers are a good fly choice. Use the boulders as cover and flip the fly at the tail of the pool above you. Sometimes you'll get an explosive strike. Small nymphs work well when fished right on the bottom. There is a fair Brown Drake hatch in late March and early April on a small stretch of river above the gorge. But, starting in 1990, the Park Service has closed fishing in the park from November 15 to the last Saturday in April. This effectively limits the fishing in the gorge to a four month period (from mid-July to mid-November). Fall is the best time to be on this portion of river. The water cools and the trout become active. At this time almost any well presented small dry fly will bring strikes. There is a good hatch of the small olive caddis and also a fair hatch of the giant orange caddis, which I've only seen on this particular part of the river. Again, most of the fish will be 8-12 inches, with a few at 14 and the rare one going to 16 inches. An occasional monster brown is taken here by the dedicated, skilled, and lucky angler. As with most places there used to be more big ones than there are today.

In the 1940s the late Charlie Brooks was getting his start as a fly fisherman on this part of the Merced. Famous for his books on Yellowstone area waters, few people know that Yosemite's Merced River is where he cut his teeth as an angler. He worked for the Park Service as a summer ranger, and one of his duties was to keep tabs on the fishing in the Merced. During one creel survey he saw a fisherman land a 21 inch rainbow near the Arch Rock Entrance Station. Later that year he caught an 18 incher of his own in this part of the river. Large rainbows unfortunately are now rare in the Merced, but there are still some good-sized browns lurking in the depths waiting for a fisherman with patience and talent. These big browns have obtained their size by being shy and cautious. They do the bulk of their feeding at night, so the angler only has a good chance to take them early in the morning or at dusk. Trout of 14-16 inches are considered very good-sized fish for all areas of the river.

Upstream from the gorge lies Yosemite Valley. Inside the seven mile long valley the Merced is largely a meadow river. The water is slow and deep with only a few white water spots. This is where the river gets 90 percent of the fishing pressure. And, 90 percent of these fishermen are inexperienced. They are mostly tourists who are not in the park solely for the fishing. They come for the scenery; it is spectacular. Yosemite Valley has spoiled me. Its scenic beauty dwarfs almost every other landscape I've encountered in North America. Unfortunately for the fishing tourists, the Yosemite Valley portion of the Merced is the most difficult portion to fish. Actually I should say it's the most difficult portion to catch fish in. It's easy to fish, with its slow current and grassy banks. It is easy to follow, easy to wade, and easy to cast. The problems are as follows:

1. The water is slow and clear.
2. There isn't much cover (for the fish in the water or the fisher man on the shore).
3. There isn't a large population of fish.
4. There is a large population of people using the river.

Most people who fish the river in the valley walk up to the bank, cast out their bait, then lie down and admire the scenery. Most don't catch fish. The lucky ones who do catch trout keep them. Some are eaten, but many are thrown away after being proudly displayed back at camp—a terrible waste of a dwindling natural resource. Nothing I say here will help inexperienced fishermen catch more fish in the valley because they are difficult fish to catch. The best advice I could give beginners is to go to a different part of the park and try for some 'dumber' trout. There are also many places where the trout are more plentiful than in the valley. The fish here are hard to locate, and even when located, are hard to catch.

For the fly fisherman it isn't so much a matter of what fly you use as it is your approach and presentation. These trout aren't used to seeing a lot of Trico spinners and parachute duns floated over them. They don't nose up to inspect each offering and reject the ones with poorly wound hackle or improperly colored bodies. They are used to seeing huge chunks of cheese or marshmallows hurled at them with one ounce lead sinkers, size four hooks, and 15 pound test line. They're used to seeing rocks thrown into the river by small children. They're used to the daily summer mixed hatch of rubber rafts and swimmers. The fish that remain in these heavily used areas learn to keep under cover during the day. They are very difficult to catch and feed mainly at night. The bigger fish abandon these areas and seek less populated spots that provide more cover. Fishermen who know what they're doing can still catch trout in Yosemite Valley, but there is no question that it is tougher than it used to be, and furthermore, there is no doubt that there are less big trout than there used to be.

Past Glory

The trout fishing in Yosemite Valley has been well chronicled and documented over the years. The original Native American residents always found plenty of rainbows in the Merced. Pictures and descriptions from the late 1800s bear evidence of the fine fishing. Early tourists found great sport fishing in the river. When the number of tourists increased it was deemed necessary to supplement the native trout population with planted trout. In addition to rainbow trout, cutthroat, brown, and brook trout were planted on many occasions.

There was some notice of the decline of the fishing as early as 1898. The report of the acting park superintendent to the U.S. Secretary of the Interior in 1898 notes that the Merced River showed some evidence of having been overfished. He recommended that no fishing be allowed in the river for a few years. The recommendation wasn't implemented immediately, but in 1910 fishing in the valley was indeed prohibited. This closure remained in effect until July 1, 1912. The reason given for the closure was that the streams in the valley were being fished out. It should be noted that the term 'fished out' had a different connotation at that time than it does today. Consider that in 1912, when fishing was again allowed, the limit had been lowered from 50 trout to 'only' 20 trout. A fisherman in the early part of the century may have been disappointed when he couldn't even get his measly 50 trout per day, but I think most people today would settle for a 20 fish outing. Also, the minimum size limit was raised from six inches to eight inches. The new restrictions didn't prove completely satisfactory, as in 1918 Stephen Mather (the first Director of the National Park Service) made a pessimistic report to the Secretary of the Interior. He reported that the fishing in the valley had been poor for years with a definite drop off in catch rates. He recommended a trout hatchery be built in the valley to increase tremendously the number of trout planted in the river. A temporary hatchery was opened the next year, and in 1926 the permanent hatchery at Happy Isles was completed.

The Happy Isles hatchery was in operation until 1959. During this period the fishing seemed good in the valley. The general feeling was that the fishing was fine in the river, and there were few complaints. Allowing for normal yearly fluctuations, the fishing from 1920 to 1960 was fairly stable and relatively consistent. Although there were many times more rainbows planted than browns, browns made up over half the catch in Yosemite Valley. Since they are generally considered to be harder to catch than their rainbow cousins, it can be assumed that the population of browns was much larger than that of the rainbows during this time period. Browns also were of greater average size. The largest fish caught in the river from 1920 to the present have always been browns. The quiet water of the valley has proven to be more to the liking of the imported browns than to the native rainbows.

Incidentally, the browns imported from Scotland (Loch Leven) and from Germany (German Brown) have become indistinguishable from each other through interbreeding. It is no longer necessary or possible to differentiate between the two types.

The biggest documented fish ever caught in the Merced in Yosemite was a brownie of 12 pounds nine ounces. It was caught on July 17, 1932 by Frank Hatch of Paso Robles, California. Mr. Hatch was using a bait casting reel, a number six hook, and an angleworm for bait. The fish was hooked near the giant yellow pine by the El Capitan Bridge. The Park Service has many photos of the happy angler with his fish. The fish itself has also been preserved

Frank Hatch with a 12 pound 9 ounce brown, the largest recorded trout from the Merced River July 17, 1932.

in formaldehyde and is in the archives at the Yosemite Museum. Earlier that same year a five pound 14 ounce brown was also taken. It was in June that Dick Noall caught the two foot long trout—also using a worm for bait. The other big year for record catches was 1924 when the second and third biggest trout were caught. At the time these were the biggest two trout, as it would be eight years until Frank Hatch's mammoth catch. On June 5, 1924 U.N. Gilbo took a nine pound six ounce brown from the river near Cascade Creek. The fish was 28 inches long and fell for a salmon egg. Just a few months later a brown of similar size was caught by Albert Skelton. On September 28, 1924 Mr. Skelton caught a nine pound three ounce brown near the Pohono Bridge. This has proven to be the longest trout caught in the river measuring in at 29 1/2 inches. No doubt a 30+ inch trout has at some time swam in this part of the Merced, but none has ever been documented as having been caught. Some form of bait was also used for this brownie—the exact type of bait is not specified in the available information. No records exist, but I'd be curious to learn the size of the biggest fish ever caught on a fly in Yosemite Valley—all of the above fish fell for some form of bait.

Fishing during the 1930s was good for quantities of fish as well as sizes of fish. People report spending their summers in the valley during the Great Depression and living off their catches. During the 1940s World War II of course caused a slow down in sport fishing, and fishing reports during that time are naturally sketchy.

In 1948 the last plant of brown trout was made in the Merced River. No more browns were stocked anywhere in the park after this date.

In 1951 a comprehensive angler survey was done on the river by the Park Service. In the first few days of the fishing season a dozen browns over 15 inches were reported to have been caught. The largest of these included a three 1/2 pounder and a four pounder. Both trout were over 20 inches. There were quite a few browns caught in the 12-15 inch class, and a few rainbows of over 14 inches were taken. The fish weren't all big however, as the survey showed that about 75 percent of the total trout caught in the valley were between 6-10 inches—a number that probably would hold true today.

The next year, 1952, the biggest trout in twenty years was caught. Glenn Gallison was the angler, and on May six he caught a six pound four ounce brown of 24 inches. This was the biggest trout since Frank Hatch's 1932 fish (which weighed almost exactly twice as much). To my knowledge Gallison's brown remains the last trout of over six pounds to be taken in Yosemite Valley. All the above fish are well documented and have been photographed for posterity—the Park Service has pictures of them in their files. It is very likely, in fact almost a certainty, that other fish of similar sizes were caught during the same time period. Fishermen can be very secretive about their

R. Noall and Park Superintendent Thomson with a 5 pound 14 ounce brown. June 5, 1932.

catches. Despite our reputation for exaggeration and braggadocio, some anglers would prefer to keep their successes to themselves. However, most fishermen are exceedingly proud of their catches—especially when not dealing with a secret spot. No one has ever said that Yosemite Valley is a secret spot, so I believe that we have a pretty good representation (but not a complete and exhaustive list) of the largest fish caught there.

In talking with locals about the 1950s and 1960s, it seems that the fishing was still pretty good in the valley. No huge fish were caught, but we must remember that there never were a lot of the big fellas. Good fishermen still took their share of 12-18 inch trout, with an occasional one over 20 inches caught each year.

The 1970s seem to be when the biggest decline in fishing was noticed on a widespread basis. Both the numbers of fish and sizes of fish were found to be smaller by long-time anglers of the river. The obvious explanation for this decline is that Yosemite has been getting more visitors each year, and more visitors equals more fishermen, more swimmers, more rafters—more everything. I don't discount this explanation, but I think there are other contributing factors that have to do with the loss of riparian habitat. I'll discuss these further at the end of this section.

In 1971 the policy of planting fish in Yosemite's streams was discontinued. Selected lakes were still planted, but the Merced hasn't been planted inside the park since then. I don't think this policy change has hurt the fishing very much. Browns haven't been planted since 1948 and still they continue to reproduce well and outnumber the rainbows in the valley.

The 1980s saw a continued decline in the quality of fishing in the Merced. A large part of this decline is probably attributable to the major droughts this region has suffered through. The first drought was in the late 70s, and the current extended drought started in 1987. After six straight years of precipitation totals at about 50 percent of normal, it looks like 1993 will be the first year since 1986 that this area receives normal runoff. Extended droughts definitely hurt the fish population. Given a few years of normal rainfall I think we'll see an improvement in the fishing. But, I don't think, even for a minute, that more rain is all that is needed. As we move into the 1990s I think we need policy changes to restore the fishery to at least a fraction of its former glory.

Present Mediocrity

The first step in improving the fishing in the valley was taken in the fall of 1990 when the Department of Fish and Game, in cooperation with the National Park Service, conducted an extensive electroshocking survey of the river. Twelve different sections of the river in Yosemite Valley were studied. This type of information gathering is necessary to determine the current condition of the fishery and to identify problems. Only after this is done can solutions be found. It was the first time in over 20 years that such a study had been done in Yosemite Valley and the results were encouraging. Although in general the fishery was found to be depressed, there were still more and bigger trout found than most people expected. Most figured that there weren't any good fish left in the river, but the electroshocking proved otherwise. Members of the Merced Flyfishing Club that helped with the electroshocking were pleased to see some nice plump browns living in the valley water. The biggest was about 20 inches and three pounds.

The day I helped with the survey it was being conducted on a shallow, rocky stretch of river near Happy Isles at the north end of the valley. Looking over the 100 meter stretch of river to be studied that day, I figured we'd find about a half dozen catchable sized trout. Instead, I was pleasantly surprised to see more than 50 trout of over six inches. There were quite a few 8-10 inch browns and rainbows, with the biggest being a brown of 12 inches. This was in a short stretch of water that never was more than three feet deep and averaged about one foot deep. The overall results of the electroshocking left reason for encouragement. Where the habitat was adequate the fish were thriving.

In the summer of 1991 the U.S. Fish and Wildlife sent a team of snorkelers to assess the habitat. One of the results of this assessment was that the habitat was not found to be in very good shape. The general feeling seems to be that the main reason for the decline in the quality of fishing in the river is due to the decline of the habitat—and not due to increased fishing pressure.

Strangely, during both studies, the fishing pressure was noted and found to be fairly light. The studies were extensive and covered over six weeks in combination. This light fishing pressure was a surprise to almost everyone. One possible reason may be simply word of mouth. The fishing quality has been declining for years and people have caught on. Locals no longer frequent the river, and even many of the tourists begin to get the word after a while. The valley still hosts more fishermen than any other area in Yosemite, but it's not as popular a fishing spot as it used to be only a few years ago. Light fishing pressure was observed during the entire study, and even lighter harvesting of trout was seen. Again, not too many people who fish in the valley catch fish.

The conclusion I must reach is that fishing pressure does not have a great impact on the fishery at this time. Plenty of fish were counted and measured. The D.F.G. estimates 4,136 trout per mile live in the Merced River in Yosemite Valley. This number is on the low side for a river of this size, but it's not too far below average. The average weight of fish per acre is well below average at 33.3 pounds/acre.

Some people were surprised to learn that the browns outnumbered the rainbows by almost exactly two to one. I've talked to people who have caught dozens of rainbows for every one brown. To no one's surprise, the browns were bigger than the rainbows on average.

The most intriguing part of the survey, to me, was the identification of the locations where the best fish were found. In almost every instance the biggest fish were found near trees that had fallen into the river. The biggest fish I've ever hooked in the valley, a brown of two pounds, was living near a fallen tree. There aren't many downed trees in the river, but where you find one you'll find trout. Other prime trout lies found were undercut banks—few of which currently exist. The isolated pocket water sections were also found to hold good populations of trout, but again, there aren't many of these areas in the valley.

At this time there aren't many trout caught over 12 inches in this part of the river. The Merced has shown potential in the past for growing fair numbers of good-sized fish. It can again reach this potential if some intelligent management policy changes are made.

Future Hopes

Starting in 1991 the Park Service took two big steps in the right direction toward improving the habitat for trout in the Merced River. I feel that the most important decision that was made is to now allow fallen trees to remain in the river. In 1963 a policy was put into effect to remove such trees. The reasons given were twofold. First, it was felt that the trees would be unsafe obstacles for rafters. The park concessionaire began renting a tremendous amount of rafts each day in the summer once the trees were removed. From Glacier Point you could look down on the river on any warm day and see what looked like the Seventh Fleet floating leisurely downstream.

Leaving the trees in the river can't help but improve the habitat for the fish. The downed trees allow vegetation to grow, which in turn will increase aquatic insect populations. In other words each tree will be a supermarket for trout. In addition, each tree will be an apartment complex for trout. Trout need protection from the current and trees provide excellent holding water. Trout also seek protection from predators such as other fish, birds, animals, and fishermen. Trees are first rate protection from all of these. The second reason given for the removal of trees in the past was that they could damage the bridges if they were left in the water. The feeling was that if enough trees were carried downstream during high water they could build up behind the bridges and destroy them. I don't doubt that this could indeed occur, but it wouldn't be a major catastrophe (in my opinion). In fact, the bridges greatly add to the erosion problems of the river. The bridges have been constructed right in the riverbed and therefore obstruct the current unnaturally during high water periods. This creates abnormal water velocity that scours the river below them and deposits sand downstream. The Park Service says now that if they lose a bridge they'll reconstruct it—this time out of the riverbed where it should have been all along. I can never prove it, due to the large variety of variable factors, but I think that the 1963-1990 policy of removing trees from the river was the single most damaging blow to the fishing in Yosemite Valley. I think it was more damaging than the increase in park visitors, and more damaging than the drought periods. Droughts have always occurred throughout history and the fish have survived. Man tampering with the natural scheme of nature can do a great deal of damage if left unchecked. I greatly applaud the Park Service's new policy of leaving the trees in the river. I'll be very interested to watch the fishing improve over the coming years.

The second big step taken by the Park Service in 1991 was to begin to battle the erosion of the river banks. The river was found to be twice as wide in some spots as it was in 1919! A wider river is a shallower river, which is a warmer river. All of these conditions are detrimental to trout. Visitors have unwittingly eroded the banks while swimming, rafting, and wading in the river. The banks get trampled and the result is that the river widens. Also, this bank erosion eliminates the undercuts that trout use for cover. In 1991 the Park Service

Fishing Merced River below Half Dome.

addressed this problem by beginning a restoration project of the stream bank at the Lower River Campground. First, the eroded banks were recontoured. Next, the area was replanted with indigenous vegetation. Finally, steps were taken to avoid allowing the erosion to recur. A split rail fence was built near the river bank and signs were put up asking people to keep out of the area. The area will be closely watched by park employees. By using such fences, signs, and educational programs, Yosemite hopes to greatly reduce the trampling of the river banks. Users of the river will be directed to certain areas where natural conditions minimize the probability of erosion. This project is to be praised.

In going one step further I feel that the Park Service also should discontinue the concessionaire's rental of inflatable rafts in Yosemite Valley. Rafters stop at various points along the river and erode the fragile banks when getting in and out of the rafts. With the increasing number of downed trees in the river in the coming years, navigating the river will become gradually more dangerous. Even if rafting is not entirely banned, the elimination of rentals in the valley probably would reduce the number of rafters by 90 percent or more. The number of people who bring their own rafts is very small when compared to the number of people who rent them when they get to Yosemite. In addition, raft owners are probably better at handling their craft than renters who may be on a rubber raft for the first time.

In conjunction with the aforementioned habitat improvement effort, the Park Service also adopted new fishing regulations designed to enhance the Merced River fishery. Starting in 1992 bait fishing is no longer allowed in Yosemite Valley. Artificial flies and lures with barbless hooks are the only approved methods that can be used by anglers in the run from the Pohono Bridge upstream to the Happy Isles footbridge. This will allow fish to be released unharmed, and is necessary because the new regulations also call for the release of all rainbow trout. Brown trout can still be kept—up to a limit of five per day. Previously, fishermen were permitted to keep five total trout of either species. It is now necessary to know the difference between browns and rainbows when fishing the Merced in Yosemite Valley. The reason for this new regulation is that there is a policy in all our national parks which favors the native species. In this case the native species is the rainbow trout—brown trout are an introduced species in the Merced. These new regulations should improve the trout fishing in the valley. Rainbows are generally easier to catch than browns, so by ensuring their release, their numbers should increase. Browns should continue to thrive due to their wariness. The two species tend to inhabit different zones in a river, so an increase in the rainbow population shouldn't lead to a decrease in the population of browns. Overall, the new regulations should lead to more total trout in the river. When these are combined with the habitat improvement programs, the future of trout fishing in Yosemite Valley appears promising. I'm looking forward to more and bigger trout from this section of the Merced in coming years.

Following the river upstream it changes character and becomes a swift boulder-strewn river once more. The three miles from the top of Yosemite Valley at Happy Isles to Nevada Fall are not fished very often. There is a good reason for this. The terrain is rugged, which makes for rough going along the river. Here there are both browns and rainbows found in the pockets and car-sized plunge pools. Most of these trout are in the 8-12 inch range. Small caddisflies are a good choice, but any dry fly pattern that floats well will draw strikes when fish are feeding on top. In this fast water fish don't have much time to examine a passing fly, so they aren't too choosy. General nymphs such as the Hare's Ear and Zug Bug are solid sub-surface producers. Many people hike the trail above the river on their way to view the spectacular waterfalls. You won't see many people fishing the river, although there is a healthy population of wild trout in this stretch.

Just above Vernal Fall is a big, beautiful pool aptly named Emerald Pool. Its deep green water would be extremely serene were it not for the crashing sound of the waterfall just below. Despite its proximity to the falls, it's a popular swimming hole. However, it's so close to the falls that I feel it is foolish to swim in it until late summer when the flow is reduced to the point where a helpless swimmer being carried downstream would be stopped by the rocks below, and not swept over the falls. Immediately above the Emerald Pool is the Silver Apron, a shallow chute of water that glistens over granite as it plunges into the pool. It looks like a natural water slide, and is used as such, but can easily lead to cuts, bruises, and worse. This big pool does contain a few trout, despite the hordes of people who swim in it and walk its banks, but it is a fragile fishery that can't stand much abuse. Any fish caught here should be released, because if not, the pool could easily become fishless. New fish can't migrate upstream to the pool due to the falls below, and the fish in the pool can't go upstream due to the Silver Apron.

The Emerald Pool is the setting for a local legend that I heard years ago from a long-time Merced resident. I have no reason to doubt the story because it took place before the fishing boom of the post World War II era when there were more big fish in these parts, and anyway, I'd prefer to believe it. It's a fish story that should be taken that way, but it's such an intriguing story in such a romantic setting that I hope it is true. I don't like to pass along unsubstantiated rumors, but with the reader forewarned, I'll tell the story to the best of my recollection.

I believe it was during the late 1930s that a couple of boys were fishing with their dad. The fishing was good in the river, as it usually was in those days, especially for knowledgeable locals like these. The

Fishing the Merced River below Yosemite Falls in Yosemite Valley.

rainbows and browns were of greater average size than today's, but a trout of two pounds was even then considered a fine catch. So, when the big fish was spotted in the Emerald Pool, this trio was appropriately impressed. The fish was well beyond casting range in the deep water of the middle of the pool. If it hadn't looked so big to all three of them they might have moved on to other fish in other places. But, this fish was special, so it commanded special attention.

A big bait was needed to get the attention of the fish, and somehow this bait would have to be delivered to the middle of the pool. After much thought one of the boys had an idea that was deemed worthy of a try. Acting on this idea, a field mouse was caught, alive, and promptly hooked through the scruff of the neck with one point of a large treble hook. The ingenious fishermen then moved to the head of the pool, at the foot of the Silver Apron, where the narrow current feeds the wide pool. Placing the struggling mouse on a piece of driftwood, with the treble hook secured to a strong fishing line, the craft and its skipper were duly launched into the main current. The stunned mouse floated downstream on the piece of wood looking like a ship wrecked sailor awash in a vast ocean. Meanwhile, the fisherman fed line from his reel to keep up with the current and ensure the important drag free float of the driftwood and its passenger. As the wood floated unimpeded downstream it naturally followed the course of the main current, which was in the middle of the pool, which is naturally where you'd expect a big trout to be. The fishermen watched with bated breath as their baited hook moved toward the vicinity of where they'd spotted the monster trout a half hour earlier. The sound of their heartbeat almost was enough to drown out the sound of thousands of gallons of water crashing over 317 foot high Vernal Fall. The mouse had to be hearing the waterfall and wondering (in its little mouse brain) how it could possibly escape taking the plunge over the precipice looming downstream. Like Bogart and Hepburn in the African Queen, the mouse floated toward the deafening roar.

As the driftwood neared the middle of the pool, the fishermen watched intently, confident that it was on the correct line toward the fish; if the fish was still in the same spot. To a casual observer an exact spot in a big pool would quickly be lost to memory while only a very general recollection of the location would remain. But, to a dedicated fisherman, the site of a big trout's rise could be closely pinpointed and probably never forgotten. The three fishermen, two observing and one holding the rod, nearly simultaneously whispered "right there!", and then, with a nod from the others, the mastermind of this plan tightened the line. The slack quickly disappeared, although the seconds seemed like minutes to the participants, and suddenly, "mouse overboard!". The driftwood floated on downstream as the mouse swam frantically for shore. The tiny mouse struggled against the current, but not for long. The big trout was indeed home, and in a flash exploded to the surface engulfing the gourmet feast. The fisherman at the head of the pool, in panicked surprise, set the hook hard and instantly. It would have been too soon except for the great distance between angler and fish, and the barb was sunk true and deep. The fish felt the sting of the hook and leapt five feet clear of the water landing in an arc of spray. The exuberant spectators screamed cheers of delight while the boy with the rod could only gasp and scarcely breathe as he attended to the task as intently as if his very life depended on it. The trout, upon becoming airborne, had revealed its species. It was a rainbow, far bigger than any of them had ever seen. Subsequent leaps led them to conclude it was over two feet long, and no doubt the most beautiful fish they had ever laid eyes upon.

No picture can do justice to a wild trout that's lived in clear mountain water, and no red is as deeply colorful as the stripe on a leaping rainbow. Anyone who's seen such a leap knows that it is an image burned deeply into one's memory that will never be erased.

The silvery, crimson, olive, black, purple and pink projectile was gradually tamed, and after 10 minutes the spent warrior was hauled through the shallows, scooped ashore, and pounced upon by the triumphant conquerors. Bear in mind that this was before the days of catch and release, so the fish was proudly carried back to camp—not that a great percentage of today's anglers would be noble enough to release a trout like this one. It was found to weigh in excess of six pounds. Perhaps a man's memory, especially a fisherman's memory, is prone to exaggeration as the years pass. But, only three people will ever know the truth, and for the rest of us, all we will ever know is the Legend of the Emerald Pool.

Above Nevada Fall the Merced flows through scenic Little Yosemite Valley. Here you'll find more hikers (and bears) than anywhere else in the Yosemite backcountry. The Merced is more like a stream than a river up here. It's much smaller than below, having not yet picked up many of the larger feeder streams. There are, in addition to plenty of people and bears, plenty of trout. The browns average 10 inches while the average rainbow is about eight inches. Here the terrain levels out and the river flows slowly and evenly.

Rainbows and brookies were planted in the early 1900s, but most of the fish caught will be browns. These browns are ancestors of plants made in Merced Lake. They have worked upstream and downstream from the lake and are the predominate trout in this stretch of river. A few good-sized browns are occasionally caught here, but a 12 incher is well above average. To get one of the rare 14-18 inch brownies, you should fish away from the campground in areas where the trail leaves the river. You also should fish in the low light periods of early morning and evening, while concentrating your efforts around the fallen trees in the water. Fishing near these trees may cause you many snags, but also will afford you the opportunity to hook the best trout.

There are abundant tiny mayfly nymphs and small stonefly nymphs living under the rocks in the river. Small Hare's Ear and Pheasant Tail patterns imitate these well when fished in sizes 12-20. Similar sized dry flies dark in color match the adults. An Adams is my number one choice when fishing on the surface. The small olive caddisfly is also found here. The same Hare's Ear nymph as used for the stonefly imitates the caddis pupa effectively. An olive or tan Elk Hair Caddis dry fly in size 14-18 is also a great choice. There isn't much fishing pressure in the river except around the campsites.

As you head upstream toward Merced Lake you will again see sections of rapids and cascades. This is truly a river of many moods. At the head of Little Yosemite Valley is a big beautiful cascade. In another part of the country it would probably be famous—here, it isn't even named. Above this cascade the Merced flows smoothly through Lost Valley, where small to medium sized browns populate the river. At the head of Lost Valley you find another impressive cascade—Bunnell Cascade (at least this one has a name). The large pool below the crashing cascade holds browns and rainbows. I haven't seen any big ones, but it wouldn't surprise me if there were some good trout in this big hole.

Above Bunnell Cascade the river flows through Echo Valley. This is wider, and longer than Lost Valley, and here the river has good numbers of rainbows and browns that seldom exceed a foot in length. The trail crosses Echo Creek after swinging away from the Merced through the valley. The lower portion of Echo Creek is currently fishless, as it has completely dried up in its lower run during the last few drought years. Fish from the Merced will probably soon work up and repopulate this stretch in time. The upstream portion does have a fairly dense population of small rainbows and brooks. After leaving the calm flats of Echo Valley the upstream hiker hears the river churn loudly again as it drops from nearby Merced Lake.

Merced Lake sees more fishermen than the river. This deep lake holds some rainbows and brookies, but browns are the dominant trout. I've caught dozens of trout in the lake, and have found the population to be about 90 percent browns. The fish in the lake will be slightly bigger than those found in the river. The biggest fish are browns, but I've taken rainbows of 13 inches. The browns average about 10 inches, but there are plenty of 12 inchers, and enough 14 inch trout to keep things lively. There are a few bigger browns (in the 16-18 inch class), but these are rare. While there are good numbers of trout in the lake, fishing success doesn't seem to correlate to this large fish population. Most people only report fair results when trying their luck at Merced Lake. I believe the explanation for this goes no further than the fishing pressure the lake receives. It is an extremely popular lake with all types of visitors; including fishermen. The always full Merced Lake High Sierra Camp is found on the eastern side of the lake. There are also plenty of sites available for tent campers that also get crowded nearly every day of the summer.

Fly fishermen have an advantage here, as at all heavily fished lakes, because they can use tiny flies that imitate the food eaten by these selective trout. I found tiny (#20) Pheasant Tail nymphs to work well when fishing below the surface during the afternoon. I found the stomachs of the fish to be full of tiny mosquito larvae whenever I used my stomach pump to check. In the evening fish will start chasing caddis pupae. Most of the caddis are light colored in the 14-18 size range. A Hare's Ear in this size is often effective, as is the more exact tan sparkle pupae. The last hour of daylight can produce exciting fishing conditions when the trout are chasing caddis. On most July nights, from 7:30-8:30, the water comes alive with feeding trout. Some very nice fish can be seen completely clearing the water in pursuit of the fast moving caddis emerging from the lake. If you have the right fly on you can hook into some of the biggest trout in the lake at this time. My best Merced Lake fish was landed during this time of fading light. The fat brown weighed nearly two pounds and was one of the prettiest brownies I've ever caught, featuring bright red-tipped fins to match its red spotted body. The trout came up for a dry fly—a size 14 attractor pattern I call the 'Bullwinkle'—and leapt three times in the twilight before it was subdued. The effective period for fishing adult caddisflies doesn't last long, but it can be exciting with dozens of fish rising within easy casting range. It can also be frustrating when you are getting refusals, short strikes, or when the fish are just plain ignoring your offerings. Merced Lake trout are well educated and can be tough, but that only makes it all the more satisfying when you get a nice one to the net.

In the morning trout will be cruising the shoreline sipping tiny dry flies from the surface. A long, light leader used in conjunction with size 20-22 dry flies can bring solid action for good browns all morning. Some of the best fish can be found near the outlet of the lake. Pods of 12-14 inch browns and rainbows can sometimes be seen from the trail where it first approaches the lake. During midday the action slows considerably as the insect hatches subside. This is the time when bait fishermen out-perform the fly caster. The best flies to use at this time are terrestrial patterns. I'm particularly fond of black flies to match the big black ants and beetles that are found in this, and most Sierra lakes. I'm so fond of these types of flies that I have developed a pattern to imitate them. My Sierra Bug works well when trout are looking to the surface in hopes of finding ants or beetles. It's a good imitation, but its best features are its floatability and visibility.

The lake was first planted with rainbow and brook trout in 1892, while cutthroat were planted twice, first in 1896 and again in 1906. No cutts are found today. Brown trout, which were planted in 1905, 1918, and 1921, have done very well and continue to flourish in the lake and the surrounding river. Merced Lake is the hub of the area fishing, and can yield dividends to those who know how to fish it.

The three mile stretch of river between Merced Lake and Washburn Lake holds a nice population of smallish trout. Most of these will be browns near Merced Lake, with more rainbows and brooks found near Washburn. The browns extend up to the Soda Springs area, about a mile and a half above Merced Lake. Browns were not planted in this part of the river, but have moved

Fly fishing amongst the boulders in the Merced River Gorge during fall.

up from the lake to this point where they were finally blocked by cascades. The trout are fairly numerous and not too difficult to catch. They range from 6-10 inches and will hit almost any small, decently presented fly. This water can be lots of fun for the fly fisherman with its many pockets and holes.

Washburn Lake is similar in size and appearance to Merced Lake but doesn't get fished nearly as often. However, at both lakes the best success will be enjoyed by those fishing early and late in the day and early and late in the season. During midday in the summer you'll see far greater results if you concentrate your efforts on the river. Washburn was also planted with brook, rainbow, brown, and cutthroat trout. The first plants of these were in 1905. Today, brooks and rainbows in the 8-10 inch range make up the bulk of the trout caught. There are no cutthroats or browns left in the lake. The brookies far outnumber the rainbows (about 3:1), but will be smaller. Nearly all the trout over 10 inches are rainbows, which generally top out at 12 or 13 inches. I've heard more than one person report catching bigger rainbows, but I haven't personally seen any. Most people catch good numbers of 7-9 inch brook trout and 8-11 inch rainbows. Above Washburn the river holds rainbows and brooks up to 10 inches. This stretch isn't fished much, so the trout are easily caught.

The Merced is an amazing river that offers some of the most beautiful scenery on the planet. As a bonus to this grandeur, the river also holds a good population of wild trout. In this single river there are a wide variety of water types available for the fisherman who should feel privileged to be able to chase these trout in this breathtaking location.

Merced River Headwaters

The headwater creeks and streams above Washburn Lake all provide good trout fishing. Some of the lakes, which sit high in the upper crest of the Sierra and eventually feed into the Merced River, also hold trout. Setting up a base camp at Washburn Lake is a fine strategy to use while exploring these waters. Most of the creeks can be reached by a short hike and fished thoroughly while still allowing the angler time to return to their established camp each night. However, trips all the way up to the headwaters of these creeks will require moving camp each night. The miles pass slowly while hiking up steep mountains at these elevations, especially when traveling off established trails. This is beautiful uncrowded country, so slow hiking progress isn't necessarily regretted. A camera is a must for this region.

Between Merced and Washburn Lakes the Gray Peak Fork joins the Merced. About a mile upstream you'll find golden trout. Goldens were planted in Adair Lake and have worked their way down into the stream below. The high cascades and mini waterfalls have kept the rainbows in the Merced River from moving up and interbreeding with the goldens. There is a good population of these pretty fish in the 5-8 inch range.

Someone with a strong sense of adventure (and a strong pair of legs) could continue upstream and check out Adair Lake, nestled high up in the Clark Range. To reach this small lake, you are required to follow the Gray Peak Fork for about five miles without the benefit of a trail. Very few people visit the lake for this reason. But, those who make the trip are usually rewarded with beautiful golden trout as well as solitude. The goldens in the lake are much bigger than those in the creek, as some are in the 12-16 inch class. There aren't a lot of goldens in the lake, but their beauty makes it worthwhile to fish all day for just a couple of these highly prized jewels. Adair was first stocked with California's state fish in 1919. It wasn't stocked again until the 1960s when three plantings of golden fingerlings were made. There seems to be a small, healthy population of fish in the lake as well as in the creek below it. It's surely safe from overfishing due to the difficulty of access.

Above Washburn Lake the Merced runs right along the trail. The access is easy and the fishing is good for rainbows and brooks to

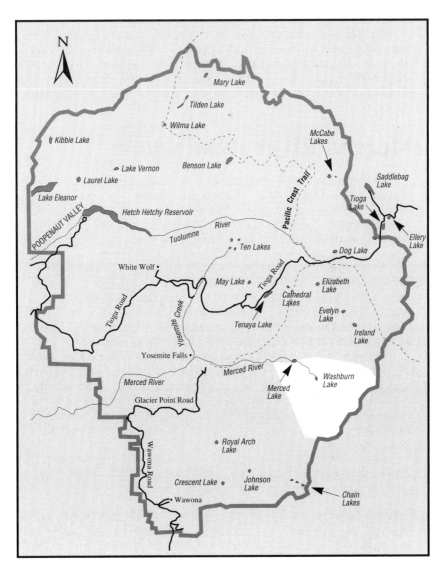

about 10 inches. As you hike upstream, many tributaries enter the river. The first is the Red Peak Fork. If you follow this creek upstream you'll find lots of willing rainbows in its pockets and small pools. You'll also find plenty of elbow room as it is unlikely you'll see another fisherman. The rainbows are typically 6-10 inches. Red Devil Lake is at the source of the creek, but it has been fishless for years. It is known to have been home to some big rainbows from earlier plantings, but they weren't able to reproduce and eventually died out.

The next branch you come across is the Lyell Fork of the Merced which also offers fine stream fishing. Here you'll find rainbows that sometimes reach 10 inches in length. These were first planted in 1908. There is no sense going too far upstream in a search for secret trout water. Hutchings Creek, which joins the Lyell Fork, is fishless, as are all the lakes it drains. The same is true for the twenty or more lakes at the head of Lyell Fork. However, in the river, almost any fly, wet or dry, will take these wilderness trout. They don't see many fishermen and are eager feeders during their short growing season.

The Merced Peak Fork is another fun fly fishing creek full of pan sized rainbows. These bows are exceptionally colorful with bright red stripes and golden yellow bodies. You can follow this creek upstream for mile after mile of solitary fishing. You could, in fact, follow it all the way up to the Edna Lakes. But, these two lakes are much easier to reach by the trail along Triple Peak Fork which leads to Red Peak Pass.

Triple Peak Fork has small brook trout that only reach about nine inches. However, the fishing is not the only reason to visit this creek. The confluence of the Merced Peak Fork and the Triple Peak Fork is an awesome sight during the run off period. Words, and even photographs, don't do it justice. I wasn't warned about this spot. It's not marked on any maps or described in any hiking guide books. The only hint of what exists is a bunch of squiggly lines close together on the topo map. Basically, the Triple Peak Fork takes a breath-taking half mile plunge off a granite cliff. If a half mile of white water cascading down a mountain doesn't strike you speechless you don't deserve to see it. The incredible series of cascades and waterfalls are uninterrupted by slow water during spring and early summer. I forgot all about fishing and just stared at the spectacle the first time I saw it. Imagine, all this beauty and no one else around. All this beauty and no one I've talked to has seen or even heard of this spot! I enjoy waterfalls immensely, with Nevada Fall being my favorite, but this unnamed, uncrowded display of natural beauty gets my vote as the most spectacular I've ever seen. It was a tough place to leave. I lingered there, taking far too many pictures, and decided that the two day hike in was worth it just to see this special place—fishing aside.

Further upstream the big, long meadow is loaded with colorful brookies. These fish can be skittish in this quiet, shallow water, so a careful approach is needed. Most of the fish will be found along the edges of the stream waiting for insects from the meadow to fall into the water. A dry fly cast so that it hangs over the grass and drops quietly to the water will bring lightning quick strikes from these opportunists. This fork is the easiest of all the headwater tributaries to follow because the main trail runs right along it for most of its length. Therefore, a few more fishermen try it, but there are still plenty of trout for everyone—they're not difficult to catch—as not more than a couple dozen people a year fish it.

Author fishing the Merced River between Merced Lake and Washburn Lake. Rob Olney photo.

The Edna Lakes sit at 10,000 feet in the Clark Range. Upper Edna is the bigger of the two, and features the largest trout. Lower Edna has smaller trout, but more of them. Both lakes can be reached by a short cross-country hike off the Red Peak Pass Trail. Lower Edna has many little rainbows in the 6-9 inch range that can be taken on small dry flies (caddisflies are found at these lakes). Upper Edna has fewer rainbows, but some of them reach two pounds or more. Most of the good fish weigh about a pound and are 13-15 inches long. A couple of bigger fish are caught every year, sometimes reaching the magical 20 inch mark. Both lakes were planted with rainbows a few times, most recently in 1969. Upper Edna was also planted with browns in 1905, but they are long gone. This elevation is not suitable for browns and it is doubtful they survived very long after they were put into the lake. Ants, beetles, and grasshoppers are good fly choices for the upper lake. Spin fishermen also do well with various deep running lures. Upper Edna is remote and difficult to reach—you don't get to it by accident—so it doesn't receive much fishing pressure.

The last group of trout lakes in the area are the five Harriet Lakes. To reach these from the Triple Peak Fork Meadows area you have a couple of choices. The first is to follow Foerster Creek upstream for about a mile until it crosses the Isberg Trail. If you choose this option you can fish for rainbows in the creek as you go. The second choice is to follow the trail up Triple Creek Fork toward Turner Lake. This

Author fishing Merced River near Soda Springs below small waterfall. Rob Olney photo.

pretty little lake is seldom visited and is full of brook trout in the 6-10 inch range. As in most brook trout fishing the fly or lure choice isn't too critical. The fish strike at almost anything that gets their attention. Turner provides a good all-around fishing experience and kicks out plenty of average sized brook trout.

The trail from Turner Lake will loop around and join the Isberg Pass Trail where it leads away from the pass. The trail will take you within a couple of miles of all five of the Harriet Lakes. All the lakes in this group can only be reached by hiking cross-country. As you might imagine, none of them receive much in the way of fishing pressure. They're a long way from civilization and off the main trail—a combination that ensures very few people will visit. Lakes one and four are barren of trout. This is unfortunate because they used to grow the largest trout in the group. All of the lakes were planted with rainbows in the 40s, 50s, and 60s. These fish have only been able to sustain themselves in Big Harriet, Harriet Lake #2, and Harriet Lake.

Lakes two and three have good populations of rainbows reaching 14 inches, but most of the fish you catch will be in the 8-12 inch range. Lake two is tiny and is located to the south of Big Harriet. Virtually no one fishes it, so its dense fish population is an easy target for flies, lures, or baits. Lake three is connected to Big Harriet by a stream and is easy to reach. Its rainbows aren't quite as numerous as Lake two's, nor do they get as big as those found in the big lake. It is still a solid rainbow trout lake that is fun to fish. Like many high elevation lakes, the best fly fishing time is conveniently found in the middle of the day. At these high elevations the insects are only active during the warmest periods. This allows the fisherman to fish during the most comfortable part of the day; which he seldom protests. The only time that fishing early and late in the day is necessary is the warmest few weeks in the middle of summer. There are fair caddis hatches at both of these lakes. Beetles and grasshoppers are also awaited by these hungry trout.

Big Harriet is much bigger than the others in the group. This shallow lake gets fished more often than the others by far, but that still doesn't amount to many angling hours per year. Caddisflies, beetles, and grasshoppers are also found in the vicinity. Most of the rainbows in the big lake are between six and 12 inches, with only a random bigger one seen. If a big fish is caught in the lake group, such as a 15-18 inch rainbow, chances are good it will have come from Big Harriet.

Only a handful of lucky people get to the headwaters of the Merced each year. This amazing river flows through areas of unsurpassed beauty while providing fine fishing from top to bottom. Where the river leaves Yosemite near El Portal, at the 2,000 foot elevation, brown trout over 20 inches are caught each year, while in its headwaters, at over 10,000 feet, rainbow trout over 20 inches are taken (in Edna Lake). Add this great fishing to the great scenery and you have the ingredients necessary for an unforgettable experience.

Along Tioga Road

The Tioga Road, which is Highway 120, is the only road that crosses Yosemite National Park. This route is a popular one in crossing the Sierra even for those who don't stop in Yosemite. The fishing waters along Tioga Road are also popular. These waters get plenty of fishing pressure—probably more than any other water in the park except the Merced River in Yosemite Valley. Many of these lakes and streams are accessible by automobile, most by a short hike, with only a few requiring an overnight backpack trip. This ease of access explains their popularity with fishermen. In fact, due to their popularity, the lakes along Tioga Road were the last ones the park allowed to be stocked. In 1971 the Park Service reevaluated its fish stocking policy. The new policy discontinued stocking in streams, and discontinued the stocking of any species besides rainbows. In 1974 it was decided that stocking would continue only in a limited number of lakes. Thirteen lakes would be stocked on a rotating basis; seven per year. Most of these lakes are located near Tioga Road, and were selected because they received the heaviest fishing pressure. In 1991 all stocking of fish in Yosemite National Park was stopped.

Some lakes along Tioga Road hold rainbows that were stocked

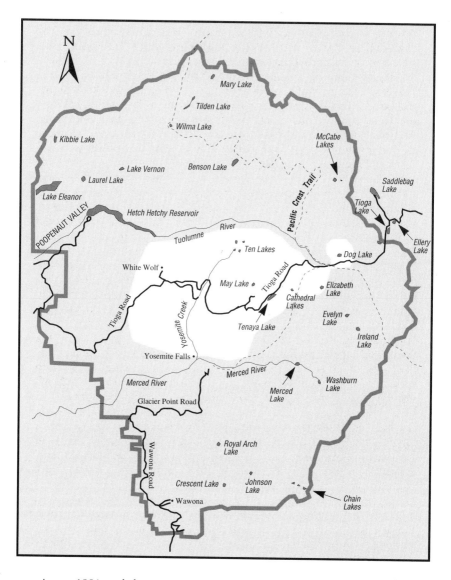

prior to 1991 and do not provide the proper conditions that will allow these rainbows to reproduce. Soon these lakes will become barren. Five to ten years is about the average life span for these fish, so by the mid-1990s the lakes without natural reproduction capacity will be fishless. Some lakes that were once known for outstanding fishing will have no fishing.

Information about fishing conditions in certain waters changes from year to year, but in cases such as this, the changes can be drastic.

Beware of word of mouth information that is even two years old. The huge rainbows that your friend's brother caught at 'Lake John Doe' the summer before last may not exist any more.

A rather unique situation is created by a dying fish population in a lake without natural reproduction that is no longer stocked. As the numbers of fish decline (due to natural death or being caught) their sizes increase. The lake may be rich in food sources for trout. When the trout population decreases, the competition for food also decreases. The remaining trout have a great time gorging themselves on a virtually unlimited food supply. These last surviving fish get quite big before they die of old age or become a fisherman's trophy. I've seen, and heard of, many a lake that is rumored to be barren except for an occasional huge fish. These stories are not myths, as the conditions just described do occur. Anyone who is after only large trout should consider finding a lake that was stocked four or five years previously. This strategy is one of the best for catching a big rainbow in Yosemite or elsewhere. There is some risk involved, as you may be too late and find a barren lake (as I have on more than one occasion). And, even if there are a few big fish left—that's no guarantee you'll catch them. Odds are that you won't, but it can be fun trying. If you do succeed, you'll have the trout of a lifetime.

Traveling from west to east along Tioga Road you'll cross the South Fork of the Tuolumne River. The road follows a branch of the river closely for several miles. You hardly need to take ten steps in some places to reach the river (really a small stream here in its headwaters). With a careful approach you can take plenty of the small, colorful brook trout that inhabit the stream. In the summer and fall small dry flies are about the only choice for the fisherman. Casting bait or lures will scare the fish in most areas of this shallow water. Early in the season when flows are higher other types of fishing may be successful. The fish here are only pan-sized, but it's a pleasant, easy place to catch some wild trout.

Traveling a few miles up the road brings you to the White Wolf area where you find a lodge and a campground. You can hike to Harden Lake and try for the rainbows that currently live there. I say 'currently' because this lake will soon be barren. It was planted every year in the 1980s, but the fish are unable to reproduce. The small lake is shallow and warm. It is very popular with hikers, picnickers, swimmers, and fishermen since it is only a few miles from White Wolf. Because of the warm water not too many rainbows can survive drought conditions. The fishing is poor and will be non-existent very soon. On my last visit I only saw two fish, but they were both over 16 inches.

Another lake with a similar set of circumstances is nearby Lukens Lake. Lukens is also shallow, warm, and soon to be fishless. It has been heavily planted recently, but these rainbows can't reproduce themselves. The lake can be reached via a very short (one mile) hike and sees more than its share of visitors. Many of the visitors are fishermen and the lake gets pounded by them. Soon there won't be any fish left, so the fishermen will disappear and leave the lake to the swimmers. Lukens was planted with brook trout from 1902-1945, and with brown trout in 1926. Neither of these species survived. Rainbows have been planted almost every year since 1942, and soon they also will be gone. There are some big rainbows in Lukens that can be fooled with small mayfly and caddisfly patterns. Lukens is a pretty little lake that is even prettier in the early season when the meadow is full of blooming shooting star wildflowers.

The next lakes encountered are the Grant Lakes and the Ten Lakes Group. These are reached by following the Ten Lakes Trail from Tioga Road. The trailhead is near the Yosemite Creek Picnic Area. These lakes are the only ones covered in this section that require an overnight trip to reach. The round trip distance is about 13 miles to reach the closest of these lakes. The Grant Lakes (Upper and Lower) are both rainbow lakes with small populations of trout in them. There isn't much reproduction in either lake, so now that stocking has ceased, the trout populations of the lakes will remain small. The fish are pretty fair sized though. Rainbows weighing two pounds are found in Upper Grant. However, I didn't see any fish smaller than nine inches there. It's possible that the rainbows can't reproduce there and will die out. Perhaps there will be some reproduction in good water years, we'll just have to wait and see. I don't think this lake gets much fishing pressure, but I still found the fish to be skittish. I did manage to land a few in the 12-14 inch range, and I saw a couple that were bigger. Hopefully this lake won't become barren as the trout do grow well in it.

Lower Grant is easier to reach and gets fished more often. The fish are smaller, ranging up to 13 inches, but they are able to reproduce. It was planted with brook trout in 1918 and with rainbows many times after that. The upper lake has only been planted with rainbows.

There are some good evening caddis hatches at both lakes, so that is my fly choice in wet and dry flies in sizes 14-16. The caddis are very dark in color. The fish were also surface feeding on tiny midges during midday in the lower lake. It was here that I encountered a strange situation one August afternoon. I had returned from a mornings' fishing at Upper Grant Lake and was walking back to my campsite at the lower lake. I saw a couple of trout rising in the shallows and decided to take a couple of casts before I packed up and headed home. I flipped my size 16 Adams toward the closest riser and was instantly rewarded with a ten inch rainbow. I quickly released it and cast again. The instant my fly hit the water two fish charged for it and, unfortunately, I hooked the smaller of the two. These didn't seem like the same fish that were so discriminating and tough to entice the evening before. As I released the second rainbow more fish began rising all around me. The bigger fish were chasing the smaller ones as the water churned with activity. I had the good fortune of being in the middle of a feeding frenzy—the likes of which I'd never seen before (except on TV documentaries about sharks). The trout didn't seem to notice me on the open bank, in the midday sun, false casting my fly line. The next cast produced another instant hook up, this time with a nice plump rainbow of about a pound. The fight of this trout didn't scare off the rest of the horde, nor did it stop them from grabbing flies off the surface—it did just the opposite. It seemed to stir them up even more, and it appeared that not only was every fish in the lake feeding, but most were feeding right in front of me. Two more rainbows were quickly landed before the commotion stopped as suddenly as it had begun. I'd landed five trout in less than five minutes on a lake where, the night before, it had taken me two hours to catch that many. Despite this experience, I still feel that Lower Grant has only a fair number of trout that are usually somewhat difficult to catch. Both of these lakes support good-sized rainbows, so they are a solid choice for backpacking fishermen. Who knows, maybe there will be a feeding frenzy when you visit?

Just a couple of miles up the trail from the Grant Lakes lie the Ten Lakes Group. There are actually seven lakes in the group that are of any size. These seven can provide good fishing if you know which ones to try. They are labeled by number, 1-7, but this can be confusing. It confused the early fish planters who failed to distinguish between lakes when reporting their stocking records. All that is known is that between 1908 and 1918 some, or all, of the lakes were planted with brooks, browns, and steelhead. The steelhead and browns no longer exist in any of the lakes. The brookies are still found in some lakes though only rainbows were planted after 1918.

Lakes 1, 5, 6, and seven do not have adequate reproduction areas and will soon be devoid of trout. However, lakes five and six were planted in 1989 and probably will have a few good-sized rainbows until the mid-1990s. Lakes 2, 3, and 4 have good self sustaining populations of both brook trout and rainbow trout. The conditions seem to favor the brookies, but the rainbows may be able to survive in smaller numbers. The trout in these lakes are of pretty good size with both species occasionally reaching about 15 inches. Like the Grant Lakes, the best flies are caddis patterns.

Lakes two and three are the most popular with campers and fishermen. The fish can be tough to fool especially during midday in midsummer (which happens to be the time that most people fish). Lake two is the biggest of the lakes that have the capacity for reproduction, and it also has the biggest trout. The average rainbows and brookies in this lake are around 10 inches, but there are some 12-15 inch fish sprinkled about. Lake 3, just a five minute walk from Lake two, is much smaller. The big fish will be about the same size as the big ones in two, but the average size is smaller. There are good numbers of rainbow and brook trout in both lakes. A small (#14) dark caddis hatches in Lake 2, while tiny (#20) light colored midges are common feed for Lake 3 trout. The first trout I caught in Lake 2 was a super-charged 13 inch rainbow that leaped four times before coming to the net. Lake 4 has good numbers of rainbow and brook trout in all sizes. There aren't quite as many fish as in Lakes two and three, but due to less fishing pressure, they are somewhat easier to catch. I found the rainbows in Lakes five and six to be willing takers of dry flies, but due to lack of spawning habitat, these lakes will soon become fishless. I didn't see any small trout in either one, and all the fish I caught were of similar size.

Due to the heavy pressure these lakes receive, I strongly recommend releasing all the fish caught. This is a very pretty area that would be that much poorer if all the lakes became fishless. There is something pleasing, even to the nonfisherman, about seeing and hearing trout splashing in a nearby lake while you prepare the evening campfire.

These lakes see fairly heavy fishing pressure. The fish get used to seeing spinning lures and baits by the middle of the summer, and are more difficult to catch using these methods as the season wears on. The fly fisherman has the advantage of disguising his hook on something that the fish aren't acquainted with. If you can overcome the difficulty of casting a fly line in a lake, you can enjoy some trout fishing at these locales.

The best way to fly fish lakes is to wade out as far as possible. This allows you to reach deeper water while also keeping your back-cast out of lakeside brush and trees. The catch is that in the cold water found in most alpine lakes it is hard to stay in the water for anything except short periods of time. The easiest solution to this problem is to bring along a pair of waders. Some waders are very lightweight and therefore perfect for this purpose. They also can be folded up so as not to take up valuable room in a backpack. I've hiked miles with waders in my backpack or daypack and have almost always been glad I brought them along. If you want to get out into even deeper water, you can go one step further and pack in a float tube. You'll still need your waders, so now we're talking about some serious weight and bulk. I personally wouldn't want to carry a float tube more than a few miles up a steep trail unless I was going to be there for at least a couple of days. Yet using a float tube is an excellent way to reach water that other fishermen can't get to, and can pay dividends in more and bigger fish.

Tioga Road crosses Yosemite Creek just a stone's throw past the Ten Lakes trailhead at the Yosemite Creek Picnic Area. The creek is small and gets very low in late summer. It flows gradually toward Yosemite Valley where it makes a spectacular 2,425 foot leap into the valley to join the Merced River. The Yosemite Falls are the second highest waterfalls in the world. May and June are the best months to see the falls at their fullest. During low water years the falls can dry up during the summer. At these times the creek just barely flows and the trout fight for survival in the deepest holes.

The trout population of Yosemite Creek is made up of rainbows, browns and brookies. Rainbows are the most populous, out-numbering the browns about two to one in most areas. Brook trout are scattered in small numbers throughout the creek and only make up about five percent of the total trout population.

Access to the creek is good for most of its length. You can fish upstream or downstream from Tioga Road, or you can drive down Old Tioga Road five miles to Yosemite Creek Campground. From this relatively uncrowded campground you can follow a fine trail either upstream or down. The trail follows the creek closely downstream all the way to the brink of Yosemite Falls; about seven miles away. This stretch doesn't see many fishermen, but does have a plentiful population of trout. The best places to try are the areas furthest away from the trail, but the fishing is usually good even close to the trail.

The quarry sought after here are browns and rainbows in the 6-10 inch range. An occasional foot long fish can be captured by a skillful angler. Most of the bigger fish are browns—and there are a few submarines living in the creek. I saw one down here in 1991 that was a good 20 inches long. The big bruiser ignored my offerings and disappeared under a rock, but you can bet I'll try for that one again sometime soon. As of 1991 that fish had survived the long drought. Browns can be very hardy and can live in higher temperatures than other trout.

Various dry flies will produce all along the creek. The best flies seem to be small dark patterns—a size 18 black ant has taken the biggest fish for me. It is difficult to detect strikes and hook fish on nymphs while fishing in small pockets and holes. So, on most creeks, dry flies are the best choice.

As you move upstream from Tioga Road the trout population in the creek becomes dominated by rainbows and the browns soon disappear. Rainbows found here show colors that lend evidence to the presence of golden trout in their ancestry. Goldens moved into the creek from Wegner Lake where they were planted in the 1930s. Where the trail leaves the creek you'll find small numbers of rainbows all the way up to its origin. Hardly anyone fishes this run where a few good rainbows can be caught.

The creek was first planted with brook and rainbow trout in 1893. A few years later an unsuccessful plant of cutthroat trout was made. It wasn't until 1927 that the only plant of browns was carried out.

Browns have thrived and have out-competed the brookies. The hardy browns are entrenched in the lower mileage of the creek providing good sport for energetic fishermen.

Down the road from Yosemite Creek you come to Porcupine Flat Campground. Porcupine Creek runs through the campground and provides fishing for pan-sized brook trout. The fish are more plentiful and less shy away from the camp, but you don't need to hike more than five minutes to find hundreds of colorful, willing brookies. The brookies were planted in 1905 and in 1936. Fishing this small creek provides a pleasant pastime while staying at the campground.

The turnoff for popular May Lake is made at another stretch of Old Tioga Road. The road is blocked off about a mile from the lake. The trail is heavily used by hikers going to nearby Mt. Hoffmann in addition to those going to May Lake. The top of Mt. Hoffmann is only three miles from the trailhead, but it gets extremely steep in the final mile. The view from the top though, is well worth the climb. Mt. Hoffmann is the geographical center of Yosemite, and from its summit you have a 360 degree view of the surrounding mountains. May Lake is an easy one mile hike from the parking area. Snow Creek, which flows out of May Lake, is virtually fishless and not worth an angler's attention. May Lake is very popular with day hikers and campers. There is a hiker's camp as well as a High Sierra Camp on the shores of the lake, so there are always people around.

Many people try their fishing luck for the lakes' planted rainbow and wild brook trout. The brook trout population is fair at best, but the fact that they can be caught is surprising when you consider the constant fishing pressure the lake receives. Rainbows have been consistently planted but survive in smaller numbers than the brookies. The average catch is usually made up of 6-9 inch brookies. Both species generally top out at about 12 inches although a six 1/2 pound rainbow was once caught here. Bait fishermen do well off the cliffs in the deep water along the western shore. Fly fishermen find small mayfly and caddisfly patterns are the most successful at matching the natural food of the trout. Black Gnats, Mosquitos, and Elk Hair Caddis dries in sizes 16 and 18 are a good bet. Small flies and fine leaders will increase success, as will fishing just before sunset. The lake was originally planted with brook, rainbow, and brown trout in 1908. The one time plant of browns has since died out. Brookies have been flourishing since their last plant in 1953.

In a couple more miles Tioga Road comes to scenic Tenaya Lake. This is a very popular lake, largely because it doesn't require a hike to reach it. Tenaya is the only natural lake in Yosemite that contains trout and can be reached by car. In fact, it is the only lake in Yosemite that can be reached by car and fished from a boat [Hetch Hetchy Reservoir doesn't allow boating or swimming]. The lake is popular with picnickers, swimmers, windsurfers, and fishermen.

Tenaya Lake—much better known for its beauty than its fishing.

Tenaya is a big lake. Happily, the park doesn't allow motor boats on this lake, which helps maintain its beauty and peaceful atmosphere.

All kinds of trout have been planted here over the years including rainbow, brook, brown, cutthroat, and even steelhead. The steelhead were planted twice, in 1928 and 1931, and are now gone. The cutthroat plant of 1918 has also long since disappeared. Browns were planted five times between 1911 and 1925 but are no longer caught. Brooks and rainbows are the only trout that are currently caught. There is also, unfortunately, a large population of suckers competing with the trout. I'm not sure how they first got into the lake, but they are there to stay. Brook trout were planted about every other year between 1909 and 1966. The few that remain are generally small. Rainbows, first planted in 1897, are even less commonly encountered than brookies, although since 1967 only rainbows have been planted in Tenaya. The rainbows seldom reach 14 inches, although 18 inchers have been caught.

A fly fisherman would do well to wade up to the top of his waders or use a float tube when fishing this big lake. A good fly for the afternoon is a size 14 caddis. In the evening, when the wind dies down and the water gets calm, tiny midge dry flies are effective when rising fish are seen. These tiny flies (size 18-24) are too small to see when the water surface is choppy. Spin and bait fishermen would be best served by using a canoe or rubber raft to reach deep water during the day. The use of bait on the bottom will produce far more suckers than trout. Ledges and drop-offs near shore are also fine spots for any fishing method. There isn't a large concentration of trout in Tenaya, but there are some in this pretty lake.

If Tenaya Lake doesn't produce, you may be tempted to try a couple of its nearby creeks. Don't. Tenaya Creek is the lake's outlet on the southwest side, but doesn't hold any trout in these, its upper reaches. It flows through a large trailless area, then through Mirror Meadow (formerly Mirror Lake), and finally into the Merced River in Yosemite Valley. Only in the lower portion does Tenaya Creek contain trout. Murphy Creek is also fishless except in the first 100 yards from where it enters Tenaya Lake at the picnic area halfway along the lake.

Polly Dome Lake previously played host to large numbers of fishermen. It is easy to reach and has provided good fishing in the past. There may be a few rainbows left in this pretty lake, but on my last trip up to Polly Dome in 1992, I didn't see (let alone catch) any trout. Rainbows have been planted a few times, most recently in 1987. It doesn't seem that the rainbows have ever been successful at reproducing themselves in this lake.

Crowded but beautiful Tuolumne Meadows is impossible to miss as you travel along Tioga Road. Fishing in the Tuolumne River can be good for brown and brook trout of 6-12 inches. The fishing opportunities of the Tuolumne River in the Tuolumne Meadows area are covered in detail in the Tuolumne River chapter of this book.

From Tuolumne Meadows you will find a series of lakes to choose from that can be reached by short hikes. Any one of them—the Cathedral Lakes (Upper and Lower), Budd Lake, Elizabeth Lake, or Dog Lake, can be easily reached and thoroughly fished in a day. A hike in, a picnic lunch, an afternoon of fishing, and a hike out, can all be accomplished in time to bring you back to Tuolumne Meadows for dinner. All of these lakes are quite popular with hikers and fishermen. If you can fish them in the early season—soon after ice-out—your fishing prospects will greatly increase. By the middle of summer it's advisable to fish the rivers and creeks of the Tuolumne Meadows area.

The Cathedral Lakes trailhead is found on the south side of Tioga Road near Budd Creek in Tuolumne Meadows. The hike up to these two lakes is about four miles. Both lakes are heavily fished. Lower Cathedral has had a small population of wild brook trout and rainbow trout from recent plantings, but I now believe the lake to be barren. Brook trout were planted often between 1897 and 1971, while only rainbows have been planted since then. Upper Cathedral houses some trout; all brookies. Brook trout plants were executed from 1948 to 1971. There was one plant of rainbows in 1942, but I've only heard of brookies in the upper lake. The trout are of fair size, averaging around nine inches, but their numbers are small. Upper Cathedral

Above: Fishing Upper Cathedral Lake below Cathedral Peak.

Right: Wading in Cathedral Lake. Cathedral Lakes are sometimes crowded but dish out plenty of scenery for everyone.

sees quite a few fishermen every day during the season, so the fish are sophisticated. Small flies and lures and fine leaders are needed to score here.

Budd Lake shares the same trailhead as the Cathedral Lakes. The trail to Budd isn't heavily used, but it follows Budd Creek so it's not too hard to trace. The hike up is less than three miles to this brook trout lake. Rainbows were planted in 1941 but brookies have taken over. The fish are seldom bigger than 10 inches in the lake and, surprisingly, also reach that size in the creek. I've caught pretty nine and 10 inch brookies that looked even bigger in this tiny creek. There aren't many fish in the creek, and none in its upper mileage. Fly fishermen and spin fishermen usually do well in this lake that has plenty of trout and relatively few fishermen.

The trail to pretty Elizabeth Lake is found in the Tuolumne Meadows Campground. This location adds to its popularity with hikers and fishermen. The hike is also short, less than five miles round trip. On your way up you can fish in Unicorn Creek, which is near the trail. The creek has frisky wild brook trout in its shallow waters. Cutthroat trout were planted in Unicorn Creek in 1896, but, like most plants of these fragile fish, it was unsuccessful in the long term. Elizabeth Lake was planted a few times with rainbows, but today holds only brookies. The brookies were first planted in 1907, and have been planted many times since then. The last plant was made in 1971. Currently they are thriving even with the heavy fishing pressure. Most fish are between 6-12 inches. Caddis and midge flies are excellent producers when rising fish are seen, while spin fishermen will find that a clear plastic casting bubble can be used with a fly—with great results. Make sure the fly is at least three feet from the bubble. Just cast it out and let it sit—twitching it occasionally. When you see a fish take the fly strike quickly to set the hook. This method can be deadly on lakes. Be sure to bring plenty of dry fly spray as the weight of the bubble tends to waterlog the fly.

Brook trout in this lake, as in many of these high country lakes, seem bigger than they actually are when they strike. In basketball terminology they "play big" as does a player who jumps well or has long arms or an extra big build. Those types of players appear, to their opponents, to be a few inches taller than they really are. So it is with hungry mountain brook trout. They hit hard with slashing noisy rises when taking a dry fly. Brookies have never been known for delicate, English tea time sips, but these fish always shrink when they're landed. I'll be sure I have a 12 inch fish on after the initial strike, but invariably the trout will be nine inches when I measure it against my rod.

Elizabeth Lake is a great place for a family picnic because of its beauty and ease of access. There are also enough fish to keep the fisherman in the family occupied while the others are enjoying the scenic surroundings.

The hike to Dog Lake is short but steep. In less than a mile and a half you reach this popular lake. It makes for a nice hike, but unfortunately, the lake lives up to its name as a fishery. There are some trout in the lake but they're pretty scarce. Brookies and rainbows are the lake's inhabitants. The brookies arrived first, in 1905. They were subsequently planted at regular intervals many times until 1971. The rainbows were planted between 1920 and 1944, and then again from 1971-1990. Rainbows can't reproduce in the lake and will soon be gone. Every once in a while a 14 or 15 inch rainbow is caught, but such catches are rare. The brook trout population isn't too healthy, but they probably will continue to exist in very small numbers after the rainbows are gone. Again, brookies don't require moving water to spawn like rainbows do. Some brook trout do reach a pretty good size—up to 14 inches.

The last time I fished Dog Lake I saw a couple of fish rising near the weed beds on the south shore. The far end of the lake, away from the trail, is also a better bet than staying near the trail where most people fish. When fishing this area you are best off to hike a mile past

Dog Lake to Delaney Creek. The trail crosses the creek in a big beautiful meadow. The creek is loaded with pan-sized, hungry brook trout. They aren't big, reaching only eight inches, but they'll hit almost any fly. This would be a great place for a beginning fly fisherman to hone his skills. The uphill hike takes less than an hour, and even a beginner should catch some trout. The open meadow makes for easy casting. Last September a friend and I (after combining for one fish at Dog Lake) caught over 30 fish each, in less than an hour, from this meadow. Delaney was planted with rainbows in 1905, but it is now taken over by brookies.

An interesting experiment was undertaken in Delaney in 1966. The creek was treated with rotenone to kill the brook trout that lived in it. The lake that feeds the creek, Skelton Lake, was also treated. After the insecticide was diluted and the water deemed safe, the creek was replanted with a rare cutthroat trout. The Paiute cutthroat, an endangered species, was brought from Silver King Creek in Alpine County. This project was an attempt to protect the pure strain of this trout. Unfortunately, the 43 adult Paiute cutthroat didn't survive in Delaney Creek, and the experiment was abandoned. It didn't take long for the brook trout to repopulate the entire length of the creek.

The Flats

At the western entry to Yosemite is the area I call 'the flats'—a term I use based on the place names found here. Highway 120 enters the park at Big Oak Flat, and soon comes to Crane Flat. A few miles away you'll find Tamarack Flat. True, this area doesn't have the majestic mountain peaks found in many other parts of Yosemite. However, everything is relative, and after climbing down, and back out of some of the creeks in the area, you'd be hard pressed to convince anyone it was flat (including my wife). Some of the climbs are measured in thousands, not hundreds, of feet, so, the term 'flats' for this country is not always appropriate.

A discussion of the fishing opportunities here starts and ends with running water. There are no lakes in the area, only creeks and rivers. Most of the elevations of the creeks range from four to six thousand feet, making them accessible earlier than most waters in Yosemite. My first couple of fishing trips of the year are often made to some of these creeks.

Recently I spent opening day on tiny Moss Creek. The trail to this aptly named little spring creek is the same one that hundreds of tourists use each week to visit the Merced Grove of giant sequoias. These big trees provide an impressive bonus to a fishing outing on Moss Creek. The further downstream you go, the bigger the creek gets as it picks up tributaries. The quarry is brown trout, and these

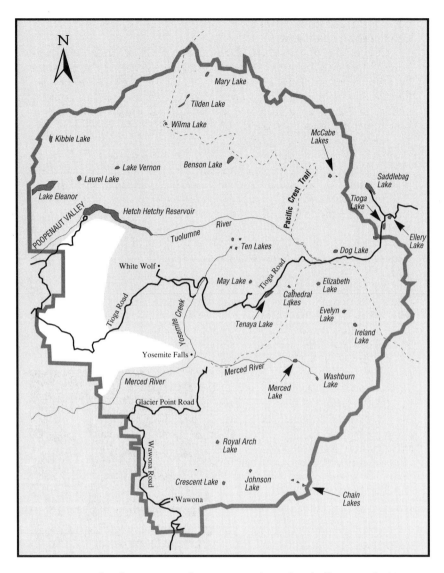

quiet water dwellers are tough to approach in the shallow creek. Tiny flies, fine leaders, and most importantly, a stealthful approach, are needed if you are to hook these trout. Most of the fish are in the 8-10 inch class, but I did manage to land a 12 inch bruiser on my last visit. I also managed to scare away a few others of that size.

If you head way downstream into the canyon toward the Merced River, you have a chance at seeing, and maybe hooking, and possibly landing, a two pound brown. There aren't a bunch of fish that size, but there are enough to wet the appetite of the serious, well conditioned brown trout hunter.

One of the unnamed tributaries to Moss Creek holds only rainbows, while only browns are found in the main creek. I caught some beautiful seven to nine inch rainbows just a few yards above the confluence, but none in the main creek. These rainbows had a bright lateral stripe that was orange, not the typical red found on most rainbows. It sometimes pays dividends to try these little feeder creeks—this one was a pleasant surprise.

An area creek even smaller than Moss Creek is Hazel Green Creek. This is not an easy creek to fish due to its small size and overgrown banks. A bushwhacking, bow and arrow casting, fly dapping, determined fisherman can catch pan-sized browns in this tiny, brushy trickle. There are plenty of trout in the creek, but extracting them is hard work. Not a creek for beginners, advanced fishermen may not stay interested for long due to the size (or lack of size) of the trout. Flies or bait are the only choices as it is too small and brushy for spinning gear.

A pleasant stream to fish that has a good head of water is Crane Creek. Abundant trout swim in its waters, both rainbow (planted in the early 1900s) and brown (planted in 1933). Plentiful hatches of mayflies and caddisflies occur throughout the year, so fly fishing with dry flies is a fine choice. The trout seem quite willing to strike at a nicely floated fly from a well concealed angler. This is a beautiful place to fish—it was especially beautiful in the Big Meadow of Foresta before the forest fire of 1991. I fished there the season after the fire, and aside from a little ash and soot on my hands, I found the fishing to still be good. The water was a bit silted, but the trout population was in good shape. From Big Meadow downstream browns and rainbows are present in equal numbers. Above Big Meadow rainbow are more dominant, and far upstream you even find small brook trout. Rainbows go to about 10 inches and the browns get a couple of inches bigger in the best holes.

Beth Beck standing before "Big Red"—Tuolumne Grove of giant sequoias—one of three groves of sequoias in Yosemite.

North Crane Creek, also called Big Crane, originates near the Tuolumne Grove of giant sequoias. This is another spectacular group of huge trees including one that you can drive your car through (the remains of the tunnel tree). North Crane is a small creek that hides brown trout in most of its shaded mini pools. The creek is overgrown and brushy and tough to follow for much of a distance. Hardly anyone fishes it, but the ones that do stick near the road crossing and obvious pullouts. Even these spots hold trout, but if you get away frow the easy access points the browns are not only more numerous and bigger, but easier to catch. Most fish are around nine inches, which doesn't sound big, but a nine inch trout is plenty big in this small water. There are some 11 and 12 inch browns in the bigger, secluded holes, but they are tough to get to and easily spooked. The creek was planted with browns only once, in 1933, but that single plant has been enough to establish a thriving population.

Tamarack Creek is a nice little creek that flows gently through the Tamarack Flat Campground and is home to good numbers of brown trout. These browns are bigger than you might expect for such a small creek, with the average catch size being about eight inches. There are 10 inch browns found in most of the good holes, and enough foot long fish scattered about to add additional interest to the fishing. A 12 inch trout in a small creek can be exciting—even to an experienced fisherman. Landing such a fish in this situation is never a certainty because there are so many obstacles (such as branches and roots) in the water that can foul the line and allow the fish to escape. I'd say I probably land only about half the good-sized trout that I'm fortunate enough to hook in these small creeks.

Browns are not quite as numerous at the campground as they are just a few hundred yards up or down the stream. In this clear, shallow water the fish can be difficult to approach. This is especially true of browns—the wariest of the trouts. The creek is tangled with willows in many areas, but a good trail follows it upstream from the campground for about a mile and a half. The casting can be difficult in the brushy spots, and a careful approach is needed in the open areas. The fishing isn't easy, but a skillful angler should be rewarded with some plump brownies dancing on the end of the line.

Tamarack was last planted with browns in 1927, and they have just about completely taken over. There were plants of brook trout (1896) and many plants of rainbow trout, but few of either remain. I've never found brookies, and have only found rainbows near the Big Oak Flat Road—where they outnumber the browns but are of a smaller average size. Small dry flies on fine leaders are the best choice for fly fishermen. Bait fishermen can fish the holes, but the creek is too small for spinners and spoons.

From Tamarack Flat Campground it's an easy 2.5 mile hike to Cascade Creek along old Big Oak Flat Road. Near the bridge crossing there are some good swimming holes which are a welcome sight to weary hikers returning from a trek to the brink of El Capitan. Fish can be caught near the bridge, but they are more eager, as well as more numerous, either upstream or down. The trout are almost all rainbows that were planted in 1935. This is excellent rainbow water with its steep gradient and fast current. Browns were planted in 1926 and 1933; brookies in 1896. Brook trout are no longer found, but an occasional brown is still taken downstream from the bridge. Rainbows outnumber browns by about 30 to 1, but the browns will be of greater size. The rainbows get to about 10 inches, and are quite abundant. The holes in the rough, hard-to-reach sections of the creek are loaded with these hungry, colorful fish. Almost any fishing method will work in these spots once the hard work of scrambling down to the water is completed.

If you hike down to Cascade Creek you may want to sample the surprisingly good fishing found in tiny Coyote Creek. You cross the creek (which is unnamed on most maps) about a half mile before you get to the bridge over Cascade Creek. Coyote flows into Cascade Creek just below the bridge. Coyote Creek contains browns that often reach, and sometimes exceed, 10 inches. These opportunistic fish are always hungry and don't seem to frighten very easily. I say this based on my first experience with the creek. On this particular occasion, my first cast into a bathtub sized hole resulted in a pretty nine inch brown coming to the net. My second cast produced a scrappy 10 incher that put up a good struggle as it thrashed around the hole. This commotion failed to alert a third brown, which was hooked on my next cast. This trout was a twin to the first I'd taken a minute earlier. This small hole was situated at the foot of a beautiful little waterfall—as fine a setting as you'd want to find for trout fishing or for a picnic, which my wife and I enjoyed after releasing the three trout.

In most of the decent sized holes in this creek you'll find six to 10 inch browns. There are a few bigger browns waiting for the energetic fisherman to hunt them down. I guess that not more than a half dozen people a year fish Coyote or Cascade Creeks at places other than the easy spots at the trail crossings. If you fish away from the trails you are guaranteed solitude, and may be the only fisherman ever encountered by these trout. At least the trout I caught acted like they'd never seen a fisherman before.

The Middle Fork of the Tuolumne River begins near White Wolf and exits the park near Camp Mather on Hetch Hetchy Road. For this entire stretch, the Tuolumne is more of a creek than a river. The three most common species of Yosemite trout are found in this stretch. Brook trout were planted in 1906 at various spots along the entire stretch, but now are most plentiful in the upper reaches near White Wolf. Most of the brookies are five to eight inches, and seldom exceed this size range. If you hike about 10 minutes away from the popular White Wolf area you'll find the river to be loaded with this Eastern U.S. native. All the deeper holes contain large numbers of the pretty little fish, which are easier to catch the further away from White Wolf you go.

Downstream from White Wolf the river flows through a roadless, trailless area after it leaves Old Tioga Road. Here the brook trout are joined by rainbows of similar size. The rainbows were planted several times all along the river. This area gets almost no fishing pressure and is teeming with trout. Below the Old Tioga Road there are also a few miles where browns are found. These were planted just once in 1897 and occasionally reach the 10-14 inch range, but average about eight. This stretch is seen by very few people, and few of these are fishermen.

Where the river leaves the park at Middle Fork Campground on Hetch Hetchy Road, it is heavily planted and heavily fished. You need to hike upstream about a half mile from the campground to find wild trout. They will be mostly small rainbows, occasionally reaching 10 inches. The population of rainbows gets more eager and more dense in direct proportion to the distance from the campground.

The South Fork of the Tuolumne River is fairly similar to the Middle Fork in many regards. It is of similar size (it is also more of a stream than a river in its Yosemite mileage), it also holds rainbow, brook, and brown trout, and it too leaves the park on Hetch Hetchy Road near a campground (Carlon Campground). The headwaters of the river are also found near White Wolf. The Tioga Road crosses two of its branches, so access is easy at these spots. The first branch you cross (when heading from east to west—which is downstream) is full of small brook trout. This is shallow water that amazes me with how many fish it contains. During the late summer of a drought year its trout remind me of dust bowl farmers trying to eke out a living. At these times the brookies will hit any fly, lure, or bait with starving vigor.

The next branch is crossed a few miles down the road, and surprisingly it holds only rainbows. This branch has a little better flow of water to it, and the rainbows are slightly bigger (to 10 inches) and almost as plentiful.

The two branches meet and flow away from roads and trails for many miles. Only one trail crosses the river before it reaches the campground. This stretch of the river is full of trout with brookies living in the quiet water and rainbows in the fast stuff. Again, it is virtually unfished, so the fish are easy to approach and easy to catch using any method. Like the Middle Fork, brook trout were planted in 1906 all along the river, and many rainbow plantings were carried out at various locations through the years. Browns were planted in 1905 near the park boundary, and today this is where they remain. The first mile above the campground looks like brown trout water and it is. The river here is wide, shallow, and slow. The browns are not very abundant, but their average size is good. I hooked only two on my last visit, one of 10 inches and one of 12, and I saw one a little bigger. This water does receive heavy fishing pressure and the fish are very difficult to approach because of it. The fact that the water is shallow and slow also adds to the difficulty of the fishing here. There are a couple of deep pools where lures would be effective, but for the most part this stretch is best fished with dry flies or bait.

A couple of small tributary creeks to the Middle and South Forks of the Tuolumne that contain trout are Ackerson Creek and Cottonwood Creek. They both have small rainbows in their brushy waters. Ackerson joins the South Fork just downstream from Carlon Campground. Cottonwood Creek joins the Middle Fork east of Camp Mather. Neither creek receives much fishing attention.

Glacier Point Road

The highlight of this area is definitely at the end of the road. Glacier Point and Washburn Point supply views too incredible to describe. Anyone who visits Yosemite should make it a point to visit these spots with a good camera. Most of the fishing near Glacier Point Road is done in the creeks as there are only a couple of lakes in the area. The most popular of these lakes is Ostrander. The trailhead to Ostrander Lake leaves the back of Bridalveil Campground, which is the only campground on the road, and a fine one at that. The hike is about six miles long and not too difficult. Consequently, Ostrander sees many visitors all year round. Yes, even in winter people go to Ostrander Lake. There is a ski hut built of rock and wood on the north shore that is used by cross-country skiers. In the summer dozens of backpackers camp at the lake each night.

The lake does have a good population of trout and although it receives a good deal of fishing pressure, it seems to hold up just fine. Most of the trout caught are brookies that grow to about 14 inches. This is where my wife caught her first trout. It was in early October and the spawning brook trout were quite accommodating. There are also rainbows in the lake, but not too many are taken. Both species were stocked for the first time in 1892. Browns are also caught, but such an occurrence is rare. They were stocked only once, in 1926, but thus far have survived in small numbers. A couple of big browns are caught from the lake each year, but they are more common in the creek below the lake. Cutthroat trout were planted in 1903 and apparently a few have survived. In 1971, a 14 inch trout was caught by a park ranger and positively identified as a cutthroat. It isn't known if any other cutts still live in Ostrander. It's doubtful but not impossible. If one remained 68 years after the initial plant, maybe there are a few others still roaming the waters of Ostrander Lake.

The only other lake in the area also had an uncommon species of

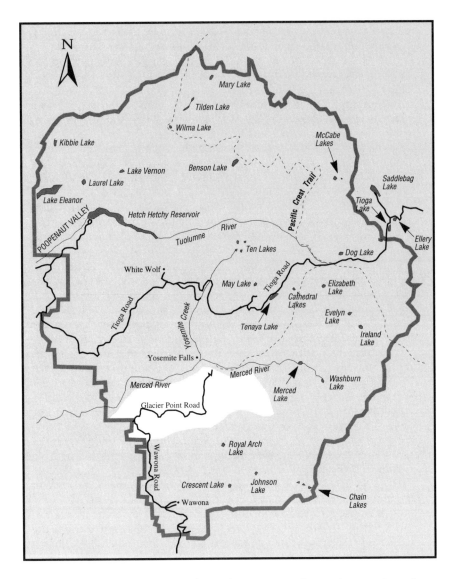

fish planted in it. Grayling Lake is the name, and, yes, it was planted with grayling—in 1930 and again in 1932. Unfortunately the grayling didn't survive for very long. Early reports found them growing well, but before long most of the grayling moved out of the lake and into Red Creek. Efforts were made to protect them by closing the creek and lake to fishing. The lake was closed in 1932 and 1935, while no fishing was allowed in the creek in 1937 and 1938. Despite these efforts, the last reported grayling caught in Yosemite was taken a few miles downstream from the lake in Red Creek in 1942. The grayling is a temperamental fish requiring very cold and clear water. It is a cousin of the trout, but isn't nearly as hardy. It is a hard fighting fish that will readily take a fly—wet or dry. It's too bad that the grayling didn't survive in Grayling Lake.

Currently the lake does provide good fishing, only now it is for rainbow trout. After everyone was convinced that the grayling was gone, the lake was planted with rainbows. The first plant was in 1947, and another was made in the 1960s. Rainbow seem to be faring better than grayling in the lake, as fish of 13 inches are not uncommon, and there are good numbers of 10 inch bows. The fishing should remain good because there are few people who fish here each year. You need to hike cross-country to find this small lake, and not too many attempt it. If you go, bring flies to match the small dark caddis that lives in the lake. There are also small black beetles in large numbers. Due to the light fishing pressure, spin fishermen also should do well with a variety of lures and baits.

Creeks far outnumber the lakes in the Glacier Point Road area. The best of these, and the most accessible is Bridalveil Creek. It runs right through the Bridalveil Campground where wild brook trout of up to 10 inches can be caught by stealthful anglers. But, you'll have more success if you follow the trail along the creek upstream or bushwhack your way downstream on the north side of the road. In the more remote sections you'll find browns and rainbows joining the brook trout. I've caught all three species from the same pool in this creek. The browns will be bigger than the others by a couple of inches on average. Brookies and rainbows over 10 inches are rare. There are fair numbers of foot long browns, and I've heard of them being caught up to 15 inches. There is no record of an official planting of browns in the creek. They probably worked their way down from Ostrander Lake that was planted with browns in 1926. About a hundred years ago brook trout were planted, followed a few years later by rainbow and cutthroat plantings. The cutthroat didn't survive.

The upstream section of the creek, below Ostrander, is a small meandering, thickly wooded creek. Mostly brooks and browns are found there. The areas away from the trail produce best, although you don't need to go far to find improved fishing. The small brushy nature of the creek lends itself best to dry fly fishing. Most small dries will produce if the fish haven't been alarmed.

Closer to the campground success is limited to mornings and evenings as the fish are more wary. It is very slow and rough going to follow the creek downstream from the campground, so not many attempt it. There is only one trail crossing between the campground and Bridalveil Fall. This beautiful waterfall delights tourists far below on the floor of Yosemite Valley. In this five miles, the creek is more rugged than above. There are bigger holes as the creek carves out a deeper canyon before plunging over the brink of the fall. This lower section holds brooks, browns, and rainbows in about equal numbers. The rainbows are generally found in the fast water areas.

It was in the section of creek above the falls and downstream from the trail that I had my closest encounter with a bear (outside of a zoo). I was fishing a hole below a small waterfall when I turned to see a pretty good-sized black bear just downstream from me. I was motionless at the time, changing flies, or I doubt it would have come so close. If I'd been casting, I could've hooked it with my backcast—it was only about 40 feet away. I don't know if it didn't see me or just ignored me, because it never looked my way. After a long minute it headed downstream. I watched as the big lumbering creature displayed amazing agility as it climbed quickly out of the rock gorge and disappeared into the trees. It always surprises me to see first hand how quick and mobile bears can be. I'm just glad I release all my fish. Otherwise the scent of fresh trout may have created a confrontation that I'd prefer to avoid. There are good numbers of trout found here, but they're not easy to get to, unless you're a bear.

The other main creek in the region also flows over one of the major waterfalls of Yosemite. Illilouette Creek, which has its headwaters in the Clark Range, runs into the Merced River just above Yosemite Valley. Illilouette Fall is not nearly as well known as Bridalveil Fall because it can't be seen from the road. Only hikers can witness this waterfall, one of John Muir's favorites. Hiking is also required to sample the fishing in this beautiful creek, as it is uncrossed by roads. Below the waterfall, which can be reached by following the horse trail upstream from Happy Isles until you get to Illilouette Creek, there are a few small rainbows found. The fish are more plentiful above the falls.

The most scenic way to reach the creek is to hike from Glacier Point to Illilouette Fall via the Panorama Trail. It's only a couple of miles to the creek, but it is all downhill and very steep. It's very easy getting down, very tiring getting back up after a day of fishing. The creek harbors lots of small rainbows in it's pocket water and small plunge pools. Please don't fish too close to the top of the waterfall. There is plenty of good water upstream. Dozens of hikers per day cross the creek on this trail, but not too many fishermen are seen. The rainbows get to about 10 inches in this part of the creek.

To reach the creek further upstream, it is best to hike down from the Mono Meadow Trail, about a three mile hike each way. About halfway down this trail, you cross the Mono Meadow Branch of Illilouette Creek. This small branch was planted with rainbows in 1950 and has a good population of small trout. A few casts may be warranted, but there are more fish in the main creek another mile and a half down the trail.

The middle portion of Illilouette Creek has some beautiful golden

Author casting dry flies for rainbow/golden hybrids at Illilouette Creek.

trout/rainbow trout hybrids. I cannot find a record of goldens being planted here or nearby, so their origin is unclear. In fact, I haven't talked to anyone who is even aware of the presence of the hybrids. These trout aren't big, about six to eight inches, but there are hordes of them. I had no problem taking dozens of these pretty little fish with assorted size 12 and 14 dry flies.

Rainbows have been stocked here many times since 1893. Brook trout were planted that same year, and are now rarely found except in the water far upstream. The creek is easy to fish and is never far from the Illilouette Creek Trail that follows it for many miles to its headwaters in the Merced Pass area. A couple of main tributaries, the Clark Fork and the Red Creek Fork, also contain rainbows but don't have the pretty hybrids that are found in the main creek.

One other creek in this territory that contains trout is Grouse Creek which originates near the Badger Pass Ski area. It also has rainbows in its upper section. Downstream, where it crosses the Wawona Road, you will find brown trout joining the rainbows. Most of the trout here are under eight inches, with a few reaching 10. The creek is fairly small and a bit brushy, but it's easy to follow and holds a good number of trout.

There are no other major creeks in the Glacier Point Road region, but don't be afraid to take a few casts into some of the tiny unnamed rivulets. Many of these contain small brook trout that will viciously attack a well cast dry fly. Among these spots is a marshy creek that runs through Westfall Meadows—a 15 minute hike south from Bridalveil Campground. The creek is small enough to jump across in most places, but the surprising little brookies offer great sport for beginning fly casters, and will delight youthful anglers. Another similar spot is the marshy creek that runs through McGurk Meadow. It can reached by a 15 minute hike north of Bridalveil Campground. It doesn't seem that there would be any fish in such a trickle, but a careful approach produces small brookies and a rare rainbow. Because of the size of the creek and the clarity of the water, these active little fish do spook easily. It is sometimes necessary to crawl through the long grass on the banks of these little creeks to remain hidden and insure success.

Vogelsang and Sunrise High Country

A person usually visits the high country around these two High Sierra Camps for the spectacular scenery. An added bonus is the fine fishing found here. Almost all the nearby waters contain trout. The primary fish found in this high altitude locale is the brook trout. Many of the lakes sit in glacial cirques and don't contain adequate spawning areas for other species of trout.

The Vogelsang region used to be the hub of golden trout fishing in the park. Four area lakes and three creeks formerly harbored goldens, but they are currently very rare—if not completely gone. In some cases the spawning habitat wasn't suitable for them. At other times goldens crossbred with rainbows and the pure strain was lost. When the two hybridize it is the rainbow characteristics that dominate, and the golden characteristics that are eventually lost.

The most popular route to get to Vogelsang leaves from Tuolumne Meadows on the John Muir/Pacific Crest Trail. Within a mile you cross the Lyell Fork of the Tuolumne with its wily browns. You may not want to unhitch your backpack so soon into the trip, but up ahead is a good creek to fish during a rest stop. This is Rafferty Creek, and the trail to Vogelsang leaves the John Muir and follows it all the way to its source. There are plenty of very colorful wild brook trout in the creek. A person shouldn't be in such a hurry to get to the top of the pass that they would pass up this fine fishing. There are plump brookies all along the lower section, and it's usually no trouble getting them to smash many different types of dry flies. The fish get more scarce as the creek gets smaller in the upper section.

When you get to the Vogelsang High Sierra Camp you'll always find legions of campers and plenty of fishermen. My most recent trip

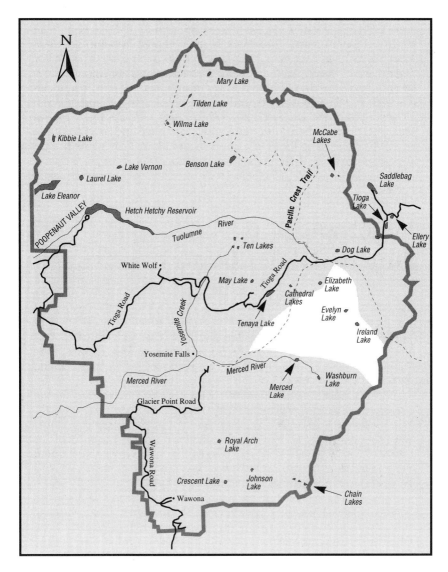

there was in the very early season (late June at this elevation is still considered early season). The fishing was good even right at the camp on Fletcher Creek. In fact, my brother-in-law caught his first ever trout just a stone's throw from the camp. The fish in Fletcher Creek are mostly brookies, and they aren't too big. That's generally the case with all the fish in the creeks at this 10,000 foot elevation. A nine or 10 inch trout from one of these creeks is a braggin' fish.

The lakes hold some bigger fish, but the majority are still pan sized brookies. Bernice, Gallison, Boothe, Babcock and Ireland lakes all fall into this category, with the brookies going to about 10 inches. Some of these were stocked with rainbows that didn't survive, and Boothe Lake was once stocked with cutthroat.

Hanging Basket Lake holds cutthroat, but their numbers and sizes are small. This may be the only place left in Yosemite where you can catch cutthroat trout. Any fish caught will probably be less than 10 inches, although in years past some bigger cutts were caught. Please release any fish caught here to preserve this unique fishery.

Fletcher Lake, the closest lake to the High Sierra Camp, is home to small brook trout. It also has been extensively planted with other types of trout over the years. Browns were planted in 1913, with a planting of goldens following in 1920. Neither survived for long, so in 1942 rainbow plants were attempted. The rainbows weren't successful either. Brookies were then planted, and they are the only trout that remain today. Over the years some goldens have been caught in the lake, but these were solitary fish that migrated down from Townsley Lake.

Townsley was planted with goldens several times from 1920-1969, and they continue to survive in small numbers. Both these lakes (Townsley and Hanging Basket) were closed to fishing in the 1920s to protect the goldens. Some goldens nearing two pounds were caught in Townsley during the stocking time period. Many fishermen try their luck at Townsley, and are rewarded with small goldens, rainbows, and hybrids of the two. Most of the fish will be around eight inches, and there are fair numbers of them present considering the amount of fishing pressure the lake receives. Townsley is probably the most easily accessible place in the park to catch goldens. I always advocate catch and release fishing, but am especially vociferous about it when it comes to goldens, the gorgeous state fish of California. Please release any that you are fortunate enough to catch. I know they are too beautiful to describe to everyone back at camp, so just take a picture before releasing. Then, you can show off the fish forever while at the same time giving someone else the chance to catch it. As Lee Wulff was often quoted as saying, a wild trout is too valuable to be caught only once, and if I could add to that, I would say that goes double for golden trout.

Emeric Lake was stocked many times with rainbows from 1919-1976. These fish were unable to reproduce and have disappeared. Now, Emeric has a fair population of brook trout that have probably come down from Boothe Lake. It doesn't seem that there was ever an official plant of brookies in Emeric Lake, but they are now sustaining themselves through natural reproduction. There aren't many of them in the lake, but a few grow to 15 inches—which is quite large for brook trout. Emeric does entertain a fairly large number of fishermen, but it is still a high-class brook trout lake.

Another lake with some good-sized fish living in its waters is

Evelyn Lake. It is just over the Tuolumne Pass from Vogelsang. This lake has a history opposite of Emeric Lake's. Evelyn was stocked with brook trout that didn't survive and now holds rainbow trout. Some rainbows reach the two pound mark and really put on a good fight. When using light tackle it can be a pleasant surprise to hook a fish bigger than expected. There doesn't seem to be a large population of fish in the lake, but there doesn't seem to be much fishing pressure either. If you're fortunate enough to be at the lake during a good hatch of caddisflies, the rising trout will give away their positions. Once located, accurate casts with caddis patterns can produce fine fishing for these rainbows. Brown trout were also tried here, but the 1913 plant didn't establish itself at this high altitude lake.

Heading over Vogelsang Pass takes you past the plentiful but small (to 10 inches) brook trout in Gallison and Bernice Lakes. To reach the bigger rainbows of the Florence Lakes, you need to hike a couple of miles cross-country, and not many people do. It's a steep hike, but if you fish your way up Florence Creek it will be a more enjoyable ascent. The creek has some nice rainbows in it, as do the lakes. Both lakes have been stocked with rainbows, most recently in 1971. Lower Florence rainbows have been known to reach 16 inches, with most in the 10-12 inch class. Caddis patterns work well here. A size 14 Elk Hair Caddis does a fine job at Lower Florence as well as at Upper Florence. The upper lake sees even fewer fishermen, and the fishing can be excellent. The average rainbow may be a little smaller than at the lower lake, but if you're like me you probably will catch more of them. Late in the season grasshoppers will fool some nice rainbows into striking at both lakes.

Vogelsang Lake, just up the hill from the High Sierra Camp, has an interesting stocking history. Browns and brookies were planted before 1920, but didn't survive past 1930. At that time goldens were first planted. They were planted many times until 1968, along with several rainbow plantings. Unfortunately, the rainbows outproduced and interbred with the goldens. There are no more pure goldens found in the lake.

The rainbows that currently reside in Vogelsang Lake are very colorful. They may not be classified officially as golden/rainbow hybrids, but they definitely show that there are golden trout in their ancestry. The fish I caught were small and still displayed yellow sides below their red stripes. The bigger fish, which I saw but couldn't catch, would probably be even prettier. Some of these fish were in the 12-14 inch range. The lake is heavily fished, being close to the High Sierra Camp, but still manages to produce a stable population of trout.

The biggest trout I saw was near the outlet and was very difficult to approach. I decided the time to get him would be right before dark, but my last night in the area was washed out due to a tremendous thunderstorm that cancelled all evening fishing activity. This was the most intense thunder and lightning display I've ever encountered at such a close range. Thunderstorms are always a factor in the high country, especially during the early and late season. This particular day I had decided to leave our Vogelsang base camp to check out the fishing on the other side of Vogelsang Pass. The weather didn't look very good when I left in the morning, so I couldn't talk anyone into accompanying me. While fishing in Lewis Creek in late afternoon it began to rain. I had wanted to go further downstream where the creek enters the Merced River, but the rain and dark clouds changed my mind. It's a pretty steep climb back over the pass, and you can bet I wanted to get it over with before the fireworks started. As I approached the top of the pass, traveling at a pretty good clip, it began to pour and I could hear thunder in the distance. I made the decision to try to outrun the storm. I rushed across an exposed slope overlooking Vogelsang Lake. This would be the most dangerous place to be during lightning strikes and I knew it. I had just made it across the slope and into the cover of the forest when the storm passed directly overhead. Lightning was flashing all around as the thunder vibrated through the ground and rocks. I stayed under cover for what seemed like forever waiting for it to pass. Huddled in my poncho, lightning continued to surround me on all sides. It was hard to resist the urge to just run the last half mile to my dry warm tent cabin. Finally, the storm moved on and I strolled into camp—tired, hungry, cold, and wet with rain and sweat. The sky later cleared to expose a beautiful sunset. At dinner that night the seasoned high country camp employees admitted that this had been "a heck of a storm—even for Vogelsang".

The creeks around Vogelsang are loaded with trout. Most of them contain brook trout under nine inches. Fletcher Creek is the most commonly fished creek in the area. It's a small creek with rapids and pockets connecting small holes. Only occasional meadow sections occur where the water slows down for a rest. Goldens from the lakes above used to move into this creek. They crossbred with rainbows that also moved into the creek from the lakes. These hybrids are still occasionally caught in the creek, but for the most part brook trout dominate.

Lewis Creek also holds mostly brookies. The lower stretch near where it joins the Merced also has browns and rainbows. Further upstream I found the fish to be all brook trout. Most of the fish are from 6-8 inches, with the rare one going to 10 inches. There are abundant trout, as one would come to my dry fly every five minutes or so. This creek is also small and shallow, so dry fly fishing is the best method to employ. There is a beautiful meadow section in the valley below Vogelsang Pass, but the fish are more plentiful and easier to catch further downstream in the faster water. There aren't any real tackle busters in these creeks, but the colorful wild fish provide entertaining sport in this scenic locale.

Further downstream rainbows in the same size range (6-10") join the brookies. Near where the creek enters the Merced the trout population is divided fairly evenly between brooks and rainbows. Here, the fish attain a larger size than their upstream neighbors. There are some rainbows up to a foot long, and a few browns that are even larger. I hooked one of about 14 inches, but lost him after he darted under a log and slipped off.

The lakes and streams between Vogelsang and Sunrise are best reached by a trail from the Tuolumne Meadows Campground to Elizabeth Lake. From Elizabeth Lake a faint fisherman's trail takes you south to Nelson Lake and its small population of pan sized brook trout. Following Echo Creek upstream about a mile leads to more brook trout fishing in Reymann Lake. Reymann was planted with goldens in 1930, but like most lakes where they've been planted, they didn't survive. However, some have done well in the creek below the lake—including one of 17 inches that was caught in 1936. There probably aren't any more pure goldens in the creek, but there are some rainbow/golden hybrids. You'll also find a dense poulation of brook trout and pure rainbow trout in this diversely populated creek. The brook trout were planted in 1905 along with cutthroat (which are no longer found). Downstream from Nelson Lake, Echo Creek yields mostly brookies with some rainbows mixed in. Both will average about seven inches.

The next drainage to the west is the Cathedral Fork of Echo Creek. Brook trout abound in this creek and in the lakes that feed it. Echo Lake and Matthes Lake have brook trout that sometimes grow to a foot long. Both lakes require cross-country hikes to reach, so they don't get much pressure.

Three lakes that do get substantial fishing pressure are the group of Sunrise Lakes. The trail to these lakes leaves the south end of Tenaya Lake. In only three miles, (but a very steep climb), you reach Sunrise 'X' Lake. Here you'll probably find other fishermen trying for the lakes' generous supply of brook trout that sometimes reach the two pound mark. I found dry flies to work well even during midday when there were no visible rising fish. In the morning and evening dries are superior to all other methods while nymphs and wet flies are top producers during midday. The pattern didn't seem to be as important as just getting the fly down deep. This leads me to believe that spinning lures would work very well during the day.

A short hike cross-country takes you to the middle lake, called Lower Sunrise Lake. I found only a few big rainbows left from past plants, and no sign of brook trout. This lake probably will soon be fishless—unless a few fish manage to come down from the upper lake.

Upper Sunrise, like the other two lakes, was formerly planted with rainbows and is now a brook trout fishery. The population is good, and again, some of the fish get quite big—especially for brookies. Some 16-18 inch brookies have been caught here. I haven't taken any that big but I know they're in there. I had good success using large attractor dry flies to catch my fill of fine, colorful 10-14 inch brook trout.

All three of the Sunrise Lakes have caddisflies that hatch on summer afternoons and evenings. Grasshopper, ladybug, beetle, and ant patterns also work well when used wet or dry. If brook trout aren't startled and are interested at all in feeding, they'll hit almost anything. Many different flies or spinning lures will get results—especially in the fall during spawning activity. Besides being close to Tioga Road, the lakes are close to Sunrise High Sierra Camp. This combination leads to a good deal of fishing competition when trying for the chunky brookies of the Sunrise Lakes.

Like Vogelsang, the scenery of the Sunrise area is tremendous. Catching one of the most beautiful fish in the world in one of the most beautiful settings in the world is what fishing the Yosemite high country is all about.

Northern Backcountry Along the Pacific Crest Trail

The country covered in this section is immense. It also contains some of the best fishing in Yosemite. Dozens of trout-filled lakes dot the landscape, and hundreds of miles of trout streams connect them. The scenery is awesome and the land unspoiled. All you need to enjoy this land is a backpack and a strong pair of legs. There are no roads in the entire region, and most of the fishing is reached only by hiking for a full day or more. Very few of the fishing spots described here can be reached by a day hiker. This is a popular area with backpackers, but due to the number of square miles involved, it doesn't seem crowded.

Many trails leave several trailheads allowing access to the region from all sides. These include White Wolf and Hetch Hetchy from the west, May Lake, Tenaya Lake, and Tuolumne Meadows from the south, Saddlebag Lake and Virginia Lake from the east, Twin Lakes, Leavitt Meadow, Sonora Pass, and Kennedy Meadow from the north. The heart of this trail system is the Pacific Crest Trail that runs from Tuolumne Meadows to Sonora Pass; a distance of nearly 80 miles. Of these miles, 55 are inside Yosemite National Park. As you can well imagine, thoroughly fishing this area would involve many enjoyable weeks.

Our tour of this vast territory will begin at Tuolumne Meadows and head north roughly following the Pacific Crest Trail (also known as the Tahoe-Yosemite Trail in this segment). The lakes encountered

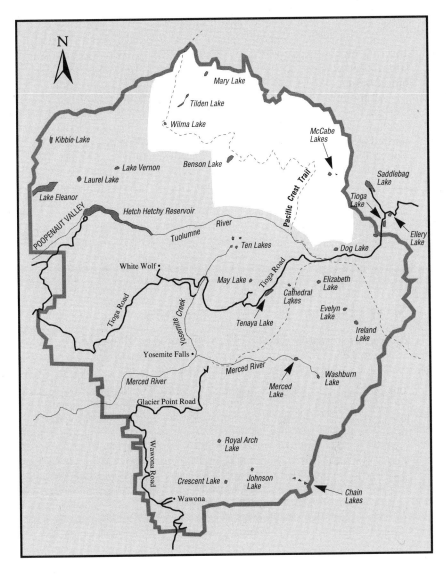

when leaving Tuolumne Meadows on the Pacific Crest Trail (P.C.T.) are the three Young Lakes; Lower, Middle, and Upper Young. A side trip of 10 miles round trip is required to reach Lower Young from the P.C.T. These lakes can be reached and fished in one day by leaving and returning to Tuolumne Meadows. A round trip to the upper lake would be about a 14 mile hike. This isn't necessary though, because camping is allowed at these lakes. Since they are fairly close to Tuolumne Meadows and camping is allowed, the Young Lakes do see many visitors. As a result, the fishing isn't outstanding. All three contain brook trout in the usual brook trout size range of 5-10 inches. These are doing well from plantings in 1935 and 1946. The lower lake entertains the most campers and fishermen, so, not surprisingly, it is the poorest from a fishing standpoint. The brook trout population isn't large, and the fish are wary, so small flies and lures on light lines are required for success. Middle Young has a good population of brookies that reach about 11 inches and average about 9. This is the smallest lake of the three, but I think it is the best. Often windy, Upper Young Lake is just a few minutes up the trail. It is too exposed for most people's camping taste, and the same seems to hold true for fishermen. I've seen many people fishing Lower Young, a few at Middle Young, while no one was at Upper Young. There are fair numbers of trout in the lake, although I wouldn't say it was teeming with fish. The brookies are disappointingly small for this big lake, averaging only about six inches and rarely topping 10. There are fish in the creek below the lake that run up to about eight inches. These lakes are quite pretty—surrounded on all sides by high peaks. The hike up to the lakes also affords some fine scenic views of Mt. Lyell, Mt. Dana, and the Cathedral Range.

A three mile cross-country hike from the Young Lakes can be taken to reach Roosevelt Lake. This large narrow lake is home to rainbow trout. Several plantings were made between 1949 and 1970. Not many people reach this lake in any given year, so if you go you'll probably have it all to yourself. Most of the rainbows are in the 10 inch range, but over the years fish of around a pound have often been caught. Many small flies are effective including caddis, black ants, and midges of all colors. Due to the lack of fishing pressure Roosevelt rainbows are vulnerable to spinners and many types of bait as well. A 'bully' lake that Teddy would be proud of.

Below Roosevelt Lake, Conness Creek contains small brook and rainbow trout. Most of the miles of this creek go unfished for years at a time because no trail crosses it. Near Glen Aulin, Conness Creek joins fishless Alkali Creek before running into the Tuolumne River. The Tuolumne is the best bet in the area for anyone who wishes to fish in running water. Dingley Creek (crossed on the Young Lakes Trail) is fishless as is the Cold Canyon branch of Conness Creek. The P.C.T. follows the Cold Canyon branch for several miles as it heads north from Glen Aulin, but only in the extreme lower portion of the creek will trout be found. There, a few brook and brown trout that have come up from the river can be taken.

A couple of lakes can be reached by hiking cross-country from the P.C.T. through Cold Canyon. Mattie Lake is a solid brook trout producer for fish in the 8-12 inch class. The population of trout is fairly dense and not too many people fish it. Most of the fishermen found at Mattie are from the High Sierra Camp at Glen Aulin.

A few miles up the trail is another brook trout lake that is reached via a cross-country hike. Virginia Lake also receives light angling pressure, but the brook trout aren't as numerous as those found at Mattie. The fish that do survive at Virginia attain a pretty fair size—especially for brookies—sometimes reaching 14-18 inches. Such fish are not often caught, but certainly offer an intriguing challenge. Many different species of trout have been planted in this lake over the years, but only the brookies have survived. Before the brook trout plantings of 1949 and 1962, goldens were tried in 1936 and 1938, while rainbows were put in this previously barren water in 1913.

The three McCabe Lakes can be reached by trail from Tuolumne Meadows or by traveling cross-country from Saddlebag Lake. The cross-country route takes only about two hours one way, but is steep and should be attempted only by experienced hikers. By trail the hike is about 14 miles one way and takes about six hours. This is the approach taken by most visitors. Those who come by trail usually camp and fish at Lower McCabe and rarely visit the other two lakes. The trout in Lower McCabe are rainbows generally about 8-11 inches. These fish do see quite a few fishermen, consequently they can be difficult to hook. The population isn't dense, so a quiet approach is needed when a fish is spotted. One fish per hour is not a bad showing at Lower McCabe. I spent a fishless hour using assorted dry flies, and didn't score until I put on a #14 Black Gnat. The response was immediate as on my first cast I was rewarded with a 10 inch leaping rainbow. The proof that this wasn't a fluke was soon found. As I removed the Black Gnat I found the remains of a black beetle in the trout's mouth. A few casts later my fly was greeted by another aerial performer. Action remained steady the rest of the afternoon with small black dry flies, although I still didn't find the lake to be brimming with trout. My impression is that there are few trout over 12 inches in the lake.

Middle McCabe holds fewer, and smaller, rainbows than Lower McCabe. The lake is reached by hiking about 15 minutes up the stream connecting the two lakes. Most of the trout are about 5-8 inches, and there aren't too many of them. For some reason more trout are found in the outlet stream than in the lake. The outlet is full of fry and small rainbows to about six inches, so it seems a mystery as to why the lake doesn't hold more trout. It certainly hasn't been fished out, as Middle McCabe receives the least (by far) fishing pressure of the lake group.

Most who visit Upper McCabe Lake do so via the Saddlebag Lake trailhead. The cross-country hike in is just hard enough to keep the number of visitors down and the fishing quality up. This lake also isn't swarming with trout, but they are present in greater numbers and are of a greater size than those found in the other two lakes. All three lakes were planted with rainbows on many occasions between 1933 and 1976. Upper McCabe was also planted with browns in 1920. This single plant has been successful enough that browns are still occasionally caught there. The rainbows outnumber the browns by far; probably about 25 to one currently. This ratio changes from year to year depending on the snowfall. Rainbows are spring spawners, and seldom face a shortage of water when they are ready to reproduce. Browns are generally fall spawners, and in low water years they face conditions that restrict or completely eliminate their ability to reproduce. This is the reason that so few high country lakes are able to maintain good brown trout populations. When such lakes don't receive enough runoff their inlet and outlet streams dry up, and the brown trout aren't able to spawn. This has been the recent situation in Yosemite, and explains why the browns aren't as plentiful as they were in the past. Regular visitors to the lake report catching 15-18 inch browns in the mid-1980s with some regularity. Browns over 20 inches and up to five pounds have been reported. Now such catches are extremely rare, but occasional browns are still caught. On my last visit I caught only rainbows, as did the other fishermen at the lake. The rainbows average about 11 inches and reach 15 or 16 inches. I took three in the 12-14 inch range, and found two of them to be unusually skinny. But one of the 12 inchers was plump and strong and leapt three times before being landed. These were all hooked on a similar fly to the one that produced in Lower McCabe, a size 14 Black Beetle. Quite a few fish rose during the morning and evening hours for small caddis flies. The bait fishermen that I talked to reported slow fishing during midday.

This lake does get fished, but not overfished. I think the harvesting of some trout probably helps the others to attain a decent size by reducing the competition for food in this high elevation lake with its short growing season. The thin bodies of most of the trout point to a population that isn't exactly thriving. Hopefully a few good precipitation years will lead to a revival of the brown trout and add to the solid action that currently exists for rainbows.

The P.C.T. crosses McCabe Creek and Return Creek at the point where they join forces. McCabe is the smaller of the two, and contains rainbows that average only about six inches. Return Creek is a very pretty creek with a good flow to it, and is loaded with rainbows that are slightly bigger than those found in McCabe Creek. Most of them are between six and eight inches, while only a few reach the 10 inch mark. I used small dry and wet flies and found them to be equally effective for this overpopulated water. I averaged about one fish caught for every two minutes of fishing, so I think any fishing method would be successful. This is one of those creeks that a beginning fisherman would enjoy and profit from, as there are so many trout that you almost can't help but catch them. At locations such as these, rookie anglers receive instant positive feedback when they do something correctly and get plenty of practice setting the hook and landing trout. The creek was planted with rainbows as recently as 1958 and 1961.

Just up the trail from the McCabe and Return Creek confluence you come to sparkling little Spiller Creek. Another high altitude gem, Spiller is also loaded with beautiful little trout. These trout are officially rainbows, but they have some golden trout in their ancestry as evidenced by the orange bellies and deep yellow sides found on the mature fish. Most of these are small trout, around five or six inches, but 7-9 inchers are fairly common in the best spots. The bigger ones are colorful prizes that are truly some of our Creators best artwork. I found myself marvelling at their beauty and not wanting to release them, although I did. While wild brook trout are extremely pretty, especially when decked out in full spawning colors, rainbow/golden hybrids are one step above them in my opinion. Only the pure golden is a more beautiful fish. The origin of the golden trout heritage in Spiller Creek is a mystery.

The only record I've found of the creek being planted shows a brook trout planting in 1905. The presence of rainbows can be explained simply enough. Spiller flows into Return Creek, and rainbows could easily move upstream from that creek which is swarming with them. Yet no record exists (that I can find) of goldens being planted in the area. This is not an uncommon occurrence as early records are sketchy and incomplete in many cases. Unofficial plantings also have been made throughout the Sierra. Possibly, goldens were put in Spiller Lake, and after not surviving there worked their way down and found a home in the creek. Incidentally, Spiller Lake was planted with rainbows by sheepherders in 1875—the earliest documented plant in Yosemite. Maybe an undocumented plant of goldens was also made in the early years. It was later planted in 1949, as was nearby Soldier Lake, but these lakes are now barren. Spiller Creek is another spot that holds more trout than you would expect. Even right at the P.C.T. crossing you'll find three or four trout in every little hole. They aren't suspicious of fishermen, so they must not see too many. They were as hungry for my flies as the area's mosquitos were for me. This is another creek where it's possible to catch 30 to 40 trout in an hour on flies. It is generally too small to fish with spinners, but I'd guess that bait fishermen would have no trouble catching a quick limit.

An uphill climb from Spiller Creek leads to peaceful Miller Lake. This is a nice rest spot where the quiet won't be interrupted by the sound of rising trout. Miller is now fishless after many rainbow plantings from 1911-1972. It's still a popular camping location—chiefly because it is at the top of an uphill climb from both directions of the trail. Even fishermen sometimes opt to spend the night at a fishless lake after a steep climb with a heavy pack.

A better choice for fishing campers is Matterhorn Canyon. The Matterhorn Canyon Branch of Return Creek is full of willing brook trout that run from five to nine inches in this delightfully scenic canyon. The P.C.T. crosses the creek in a peaceful meadow that is a popular camping site. Fly fishermen can catch their fill of brookies on any fly in any spot, while spin fishermen seek out the deeper holes to pull out these colorful fish. On my last trip through the area I met two different fishing parties that thought they were catching golden trout in this creek. The confusion arises because the bellies of these brookies are such a bright orange-golden color. Brook trout were planted in 1905, and have thrived to a great degree. You'll find them lined up like cord wood waiting for dry flies the entire length of the canyon.

Wilson Creek was also planted with brook trout in 1905. The little brook trout in this pretty little creek run up to nine inches. Their numbers are good although they aren't as plentiful as their neighbors in the Matterhorn Canyon Branch. This is a good spot to take what I call "a brook trout break". This is where I take off my backpack to rest my shoulders and legs by fly casting and scrambling along a creek. My wife calls it "foolishness" and doesn't quite understand why I don't rest during a rest stop. However, catching trout somehow rejuvenates me and prepares me for the rigors of the trail ahead.

In this particular case, when following the P.C.T. from south to north, you'll need plenty of physical and mental freshness for Benson Pass. It's a long steady climb that gets very steep at times. Don't wait too long to fish Wilson Creek on your way up the pass, as no brookies are found above the 9,000 foot level—although there is plenty of water in which to fill your canteen. I passed many bone weary backpackers on my way up the pass including one that stared right at me with a very serious look on his face and said with some desperation "this pass is killing me". I also passed a guy with a full size cast iron skillet dangling from the back of his pack. He reminded me of a convict dragging a ball and chain. The topper though, was the group of exhausted cub scouts I overtook while they rested on the trail. As on most passes, each hiker travelling in the opposite direction was met with the standard "how much further to the top?" question. When I reached the scouts, two spry middle-aged nuns were coming toward us down the trail. As the young boys asked the usual question of the sisters, they seemed embarrassed by their own pitiful appearance as contrasted by the lively stepping pair of nuns. Boys have always delighted in insulting each others stamina by calling one another an "old woman". These 'old women' winked at me as they delighted in telling the boys that it was about another mile and a half, very, very steep, and that they praised God they were heading downhill and not up. I thought for a second that there was going to be a mugging, as the scouts, in a very un-scout like moment, registered their disapproval toward the pair. Probably the nuns were saved from harm because the boys had no energy left to expend. The scoutmaster told the group that if they had been more physically active in their young lives, instead of sitting around playing video games all day, they could have saved themselves this humiliation. Perhaps a good life-long lesson in physical fitness had just been taught by the nuns.

After crossing Benson Pass you enter the heart of Yosemite's northern backcountry. It takes at least two full days of hiking to reach this region from any direction. I consider this group of lakes to be among the finest fishing lakes in the park. People do visit this area, and a good percentage of the visitors are fishermen, but the sheer time and difficulty required to get to the region keep their numbers at an acceptable level. And because of snow, almost all the visitors come in July and August. The remainder of the year the fish have a chance to rest and eat without being harassed by fishermen.

The main focus of this area is on the lakes because that is where the biggest fish are found, and some are quite big indeed. Small rainbows are found in the Rodgers Canyon Branch of Register Creek, and 5-8 inch brookies are commonly caught in Paiute Creek, but most people who come here to fish will be found trying their luck in one of the lakes. The most popular lakes are Benson and Smedberg, but four others in the area also hold trout. Two of these are reached by trail—Rodgers and Neall—while two are reached by hiking cross-country—Tallulah and Doe. Additionally, there are two other lakes that formerly held trout, but no longer do. These are Sister Lake and Surprise Lake, both near Smedberg Lake. They were stocked with rainbows from 1948 until 1972 and yielded fine catches of two pound trout during that period.

Not many fishermen reach either Tallulah or Doe lakes. These were planted with rainbows several times during the 1940s, 1950s, and 1960s, with the last plant in each being carried out in 1970. Neither of these lakes has a very large population of trout, but they both have reproducing fish in their waters, as evidenced by the fact that rainbows are still present more than 20 years after the last plant. Doe houses a small population of rainbows that get about a foot long. If the fish are found they can be enticed to strike as they don't see too many fishermen per year. Tallulah Lake also features a small population of rainbows, although they get slightly bigger than those of Doe, occasionally reaching the 14 inch mark. These trout seem to stay deep in the water. I say this not just because our spin fishing counterparts outfished those of us using flies two to 1, but also because the fish were not very colorful. These are silvery trout that had some anglers thinking they may be lake trout, but the real answer is that trout take on the color of their environment. The Tallulah Lake rainbows probably stay out of the shallows and the sunlight, thus they never attain much color.

The remaining four lakes in this land of fine fishing can all be reached by trail. The least popular of the four are Rodgers and Neall Lakes, both of which offer solid rainbow action.

Neall Lake is small and deep and has a fair population of nine to 14 inch trout. It was planted with rainbows five times between 1930 and 1969. If you fish this pretty lake the chances are you will be alone which is good because it couldn't stand up to much fishing pressure. I strongly recommend releasing any fish caught at Neall to ensure that the population doesn't get depleted. I found a #14 Elk Hair Caddis to be an excellent fish taker in midafternoon.

As I was taking a swim in the lake it wasn't hard for me to imagine that it was all mine. I was the only one on the lake and there was no evidence (such as litter) of other visitors. As I lay on a rock letting the sun dry me, I imagined having a little cabin tucked back in the trees. I'd keep a trout or two a day for my needs, and hike and fish and explore the surrounding area all summer. Just then, as I was dozing off, a cool wind came up and reminded me that I hadn't quite imagined what a winter would be like at 9,200 feet. Nevertheless, I have very pleasant memories of Neall Lake.

Rodgers Lake is a bigger version of Neall Lake. It also has a good, but not dense, population of trout, and it also gets fished, but not fished very hard. The rainbows found in Rodgers were planted first in 1907, last in 1970, with a few plantings in between. Like Neall, the fish seem to reproduce fairly well, but the population can't be categorized as thriving. Browns were also planted once, in 1907, but they haven't survived. The rainbows run up to about 16 inches, while averaging about a foot in length. They can be tough to approach on the shallow sandy flats that make up much of the shore of the lake. It is sight fishing in these spots, much like trying to locate tailing bonefish in the saltwater flats. Because the fish spend much of their time on the yellow sand in shallow water, Rodgers Lake rainbows are finely colored. Most of the fish have butter yellow bellies, and some have gorgeous red cheeks and sides. Don't forget your good camera when you fish it (I didn't forget mine, I just didn't want to carry it for the 80 mile trip. I settled for a pocket camera and resulting pictures that didn't do justice to the fish).

The flies I found most successful on Rodgers were size 14 and 16 caddis patterns of a dark color. I also had some success with grasshopper patterns in the afternoon when the breeze came up. When it's windy a good tip when looking for rising trout is to look for air bubbles on the surface. When it gets windy and the surface gets choppy, you may not be able to see the telltale rings of rising fish, nor can you see below the surface to see the fish themselves. In a lake such as Rodgers where there aren't hordes of fish, blind casting isn't very effective. At times like these you need to find specific fish and make well planned casts. If it's windy you may have a hard time locating the trout. In such instances often the trout will give away their locations by leaving bubbles on the surface when they rise for floating insects. Just cast your fly amongst the bubbles and often you will be rewarded with a slashing rise from a fearless trout. The trout feel safe at these times because they know they can't be spotted from above. A big trout knows he faces no danger in the water, so if he feels safe from predators outside the water, he is as bold as he's ever going to get. This is the same way a big fish acts when the sun goes down and he feels he can no longer be seen. So, the wind doesn't have to spoil the fishing, and your companions may wonder how you are managing to catch all the fish.

The two most popular lakes in the area are Smedberg and Benson. Their popularity is partly due to their location—both being in close proximity to the P.C.T., partly due to their size—both lakes are large and can accommodate several groups of campers, and partly due to their fishing reputation—both lakes hold large populations of large trout.

Smedberg Lake is right on the P.C.T. and is a natural stopping point for backpackers who have struggled over Benson Pass or have sweated up from Benson Lake. Smedberg is a fine rainbow trout lake. I've taken rainbows up to 16 inches and have seen some swimming in the lake that were bigger. The average rainbow caught will be in the neighborhood of 12 inches, and they fight well.

There are abundant trout in the lake, but they aren't always easy to catch because they are accustomed to seeing a few fishermen a day during the summer. During the middle of the day, and even mornings and evenings, I found it necessary to use a long leader (12 feet) and a fine tippet (6X or 5X) to fool these rainbows with any consistency. River fishermen may think that 6X tippet is too light to land a 16 inch trout, but often you can get away with using a lighter line in a lake than you can in a river. The reason for this is that a good-sized trout in a river will use the current to its advantage. The water's drag will make the fish feel much heavier and put more strain on the line—causing it to break easier. In the still water of a lake the trout has no such advantage working for it, and once hooked, the percentages swing more favorably toward the angler. However, on the smoother surface of a lake, a fishing line is more easily spotted by the trout, hence the need to go to a lighter line to trick the fish into striking. All in all it's probably a wash. A 16 inch river fish hooked on a 5X tippet probably has about the same chance of escaping as a 16 incher in a lake that is hooked on 6X tippet. Also a 16 inch river fish is probably as easily fooled with a 5X tippet as the same fish in a lake is correspondingly fooled with a 6X tippet. There are other variables to take into account, but the point is that generally you will need, and can get away with, a lighter line when lake fishing.

Another tip for lake fishing, and one that doesn't require as long winded an explanation as the argument for a lighter line, concerns one of the cardinal rules of fishing—keep your shadow off the water. Nothing will send trout scurrying for the depths as fast as seeing a shadow flash across the surface. They may not know what it is, but they don't want to stick around and find out. If the fish are evenly distributed around the lake, as I found them to be at Smedberg, simply fish your way around the lake while keeping the sun in your face. This does make it a bit more difficult to see the fish and watch your line, but it will keep your shadow off the water and will probably result in an increased catch for you.

The hard fighting, leaping rainbows of Smedberg were planted many times from 1934 to 1972. There was an earlier (1905) attempt to establish brook trout in the lake that was unsuccessful for some reason. I would guess that the rainbows have just outcompeted the brookie, and today no brook trout remain.

I found several flies to be effective at Smedberg, all of them small. A #18 cream mayfly hatches on the lake, as do even smaller midges. The fish feed steadily all day on these tiny midges, and flies of size 20 or 22 are needed to match them. As I said, the trout can be choosy, so a close copy of the natural is often required. As such, I found a Turkey Wing Caddis to work better than the more general Elk Hair Caddis when matching the evening hatch of small black caddisflies. Sizes 14 and 16 seemed to work best at this time. Another fly fisherman at the lake had limited success with larger attractor patterns such as a #10 Royal Wulff and a #12 Adams. He caught only a couple of 6-8 inch trout, and was frustrated. There are times though, such as early morning and late evening, when large flies and spinning lures will produce. In the middle of the day a non-fly fisherman would do better with bait than with spinners. Smedberg has abundant fish and many of those fish are over a pound. The trout are colorful and hard fighting. By combining the fishing opportunities with the fine uncrowded camping spots found along its shore, it's not hard to understand why Smedberg is one of my favorite backcountry lakes.

Another tremendous fishing opportunity awaits the backpacking angler at Benson Lake. This large deep lake hosts more fishermen than any other lake in the region. Is it fished out? Not a chance—it's too big, and, though it does get more fishing pressure than any other backcountry lake around, this still doesn't amount to more than a half dozen fishermen per day during the summer. Furthermore, 90% of those who fish it hit only the easy spots. The campsites are along the northeast shore where the trail leads to the lake, and this sandy shore is where most people's fishing efforts take place. This shore is as fine a beach as you'll find in the high country, but it isn't the best place to fish.

Benson Lake has many large rainbows roaming its waters, but most of them are found on the far side of the lake. This is unfortunate, for reaching the far shore is not an easy affair. If you come in by horseback to fish Benson, I'd suggest that you pack a small inflatable raft if you can find the room for it. Otherwise you'll have to do as I did, and as all backpacking fishermen do if they wish to sample the best fishing that the lake has to offer—namely, risk your life by hiking around the lake. Following the lake shore is by no means easy. Large cliffs block your progress and you are forced to climb over and around them—sometimes far back from the lake. About one and a 1/2 hours of tedious bushwhacking, tough scrambling, and dangerous mountain climbing takes a fearless, athletic fisherman to the far shore. As you might imagine not many people make the trip—and I don't blame them at all. At the very least, a fisherman should attempt to make it part way around the lake to reach largely unfished places. Fishing the sandy shore does yield trout, but they are generally smaller than those found in the rest of the lake. The rainbows caught at the near shore are usually in the 8-12 inch range. This is also the only place where the lakes' brook trout are found. The brookies hang out near the inlet, but are somewhat small—averaging around nine inches. The brookies were planted in 1895, and have managed to survive in small numbers in a limited part of the lake. Rainbows were put in as early as 1883 and again in 1905. Browns were also planted in 1905 but they didn't survive. I'd guess that there were some big browns in this big lake, but I've heard no stories nor seen any documentation about their presence in the early 1900s. Now, the only stories are about big rainbows. They reach 20 inches in length and four pounds in weight. Fish of 16-18 inches are not at all uncommon.

On my last trip I slowly picked my way around the lake, pausing occasionally to make some casts into the protected coves where the water was less affected by the wind. I picked up consistent numbers of rainbows in the 10-14 inch range from each likely spot. The action was good, and I hadn't even gotten serious about my fishing yet. I was using dry flies—Elk Hair Caddis and Adams patterns in sizes 12 and 14—casting mostly for marked fish that I'd observed from the rocky cliffs that ring the shoreline.

As I found myself getting close to the far side of the lake, rumored home of the big rainbows, I began to concentrate on fishing. I took off my pack and decided to spend more time casting and less time hiking. As I gazed into the water while arranging my equipment I spotted a good trout finning in the shallows right in front of me. I waited until it turned away and then softly delivered my Elk Hair Caddis a foot to its left. The trout instantly grabbed my offering and, upon feeling unexpected resistance, broke the surface shattering the calm water of the cove. Two more leaps and bullish head shaking tired the fish enough that I, armed with delicate 6X tippet, was able to finally gain the upper hand and lead the two pound rainbow to shore. I then went through the ritual a fly fisherman performs after landing a nice trout. After a quick picture session I nursed the tired fish back to health by gently moving it through the water until a strong thrust of its tail propelled it to freedom. The waterproof camera was returned to my upper vest pocket, I rinsed my hands in the lake, and cleaned the fish slime off the fly. I then dried the fly by pressing it into my shirt sleeve and making a few false casts. When I was satisfied that it would float, I was again ready to fish. The above process doesn't really take long, probably just a few minutes from the time the fish is landed until the time the fisherman has put all the pieces back together and is ready to resume the search for the next fish. After such a battle with a good-sized fish I naturally assumed that I would have to move far away from this spot to find undisturbed water. Before moving on I shot a quick glance to the place where I'd spotted the big rainbow, perhaps because some movement had caught my eye. I did a double take as I saw another big trout swimming toward me. Was this the same fish I had just released? Not likely I thought, as that fish was stunned and headed for the depths to regain its composure. I flipped a cast a few yards in front of the oncoming trout and waited in anticipation as the fish approached my floating fly. Without hesitation the trout sucked in the fake and I was treated to an instant replay of the battle I'd enjoyed just minutes earlier. The second rainbow was even bigger than the first, registering a solid two and a 1/2 pounds on my net scale. I remember thinking "Okay, I don't have to look for them, they're coming to me." After regrouping I stared at the water half expecting to see another fish come along, but still surprised when I did. This one was much smaller, but a very game and extremely colorful one pounder nonetheless. The fishing was ridiculously easy for this 15 minute period—three trout, all over a pound, in three casts—maybe this is what Alaska fishing is like. I waited a few more minutes, but no more trout entered my trap, and I was forced back into the reality of having to work a little bit for my fish. I've since concluded that these three trout were prowling the shoreline at intervals spaced just far enough apart that they hadn't heard the commotion caused by the fight of the fish in front of them. The lesson to be learned is that if you are in a good spot on a lake, you may indeed be able to relax and wait for the fish to find you rather than vice versa.

After I moved on to try other parts of the lake I caught a few more fine rainbows in the 14-16 inch range on dry flies. I also spotted a few awesome Benson rainbows close to the 20 inch mark. One I lured to the surface using a grasshopper pattern, but I missed his strike. He charged out of the depths and seemed to grow and grow as he neared my fly. The one or two seconds that I watched his enlarging ascent seemed to take an eternity and I guess I couldn't restrain myself and struck too soon. I'd like to believe that he changed his mind and struck short, but I haven't been able to convince myself of that.

I thought I saw the biggest fish of the lake—25 or 30 inches—roll near the surface about 30 yards out. As I was trying to decide a couple of things, first, if I had really seen it, and second, how I was going to reach it with a cast, it came to the surface again and both problems were solved simultaneously. No, this wasn't the monster trout of Benson Lake, but rather an otter searching for a few trout of its own.

Later, another huge trout (that was really a trout) followed a big streamer I had cast into the deep water. Although he followed it for several yards right up to the shore, he never tried to strike at it. Perhaps it was a little too big and colorful for his taste. Spin fishermen may experience similar refusals, but in this big deep lake spinning gear would be a good method to use to present a lure to many big trout.

A proven method for the taking of large Benson rainbows involves the use of bait. Not just any bait, but a special bait that is somewhat of a local secret. The trail crew that is stationed at Benson during the summer is credited with discovering this secret. While cutting vast amounts of firewood they sometimes come across the larvae of the destructive bark beetle. This pest is well known for the havoc it wreaks on the trees of the Sierra. An enterprising fishing member of the trail crew put this larvae to good use one day by impaling it on a hook and dangling it in the depths of Benson Lake. This bait has now built a good following among local Benson Lake fishermen as the number one method for catching big trout.

Although Benson yielded plenty of fish to my dry flies, I would say it is a better lure and bait lake—largely because of its depth and rough surface. The lake gets windy, making surface flies hard to see for both the fish and the fisherman. The dry fly fisherman then must seek out the quiet coves, but these are hard to reach. I'm sure I spent just as much time hiking and scrambling around the lake as I did fishing it. There are good insect hatches, caddis and mayflies, along with plenty of terrestrials, grasshoppers and ants, so fly fishermen can do well at Benson if they're willing to work for their fish.

When I woke up from a good night of pleasant dreaming on the shore of Benson Lake, I looked out of my tent to the three greatest sights a backpacking fisherman could hope to see in the morning: clear skies, rising trout, and bear-bagged food hanging undisturbed. I spent an hour fishing to the morning risers and received a happy send-off. I landed a few rainbows, including a fine green sided 15 incher which I decided would be a good final fish. As I was packing up camp I thought that if a bear had indeed gotten all my food, I'd have had to somehow been able to subsist on the 60 pounds of trout that I'd caught in three days at Benson and Smedberg Lakes. I'd caught and released about 30 fish over a foot long. I generally consider 12 inches to be a good trout, although many of these 10 and 11 inchers put up a good tussle and were definitely worthwhile. I think these lakes, which are so hard to get to (a minimum of two days in, two days out) should remain fine fisheries for many generations. There are plenty of big wild trout in the Benson-Smedberg area. When you add this to the difficult access that exists, it is easy to see why this remains one of the finest fishing destinations in the Yosemite backcountry.

My wife says that I tend to hike farther and faster when I sense trout ahead. She says the closer I get to a fishing destination the faster I walk. I don't doubt her, but I'm seldom aware of this change in my pace, as I'm probably too preoccupied with fishing thoughts to notice. However, I must admit that I lost a little spring in my step as I was hiking away from those big Benson rainbows.

There are other good trout-filled lakes and creeks to the north of Benson Lake along the P.C.T., and there are some in the region that contain no trout. The group of lakes south of Benson features only fair fishing. Saddle Horse Lake is barren, and Table Lake may be also. I haven't seen any fish at Table, but I did talk to a hiker who claims to have caught a respectable rainbow in it in 1992. Irwin Bright seems to have a decent rainbow population, with the fish running up to 15 inches. Rainbows were stocked there in 1912 and in 1958.

After climbing up from Benson Lake and reaching Seavey Pass, the P.C.T. follows Rancheria Creek through Kerrick Canyon. The small rainbows caught there were originally planted in 1906. Brook trout were planted in 1905, and exist in the upper reaches of the creek. Three more fine creeks cross the trail before eventually flowing into Rancheria Creek. The Thompson Canyon Branch and the Stubblefield Canyon Branch provide solitary fishing for pretty rainbows. Following either of these creeks upstream just a few hundred yards will take a fisherman to virtually unfished water in a beautiful setting. Tilden Canyon Creek also holds rainbows, but the trail along it ensures that it does occasionally get fished. Rainbows in these high elevation creeks rarely exceed eight inches, and average only about six. Down Tilden Canyon Creek and off the trail is fishless Avonelle Lake. This is one of the tragedies of the non-stocking philosophy employed by the National Park Service. Although overall I do agree with the philosophy, sometimes it's sad to see an excellent trout lake die out. Avonelle was known as a fine producer of large rainbows. It was stocked in 1932, 1942, 1967, and 1972, and its fish grew large quickly. A 1958 ranger-led party reported catching 16-24 inch rainbows from Avonelle; it always seemed to have produced fine catches, but no more.

A lake that is still producing trout is Wilma Lake (also called Wilmer Lake). This lake is right on the P.C.T., therefore it is popular with campers, and it also yeilds good-sized rainbows. Though not teeming with trout, Wilma does have a decent population and will begrudgingly kick out rainbows in the 15-18 inch range. It was planted sometime before 1913, and since then the rainbows have done nicely.

The lake is a little deceiving. It isn't very big, and most of it is shallow. It looks like a good bet to produce eight to 10 inch trout. In reality, I've seen a few rainbows twice that size cruising its shallow shoreline. One fish in particular stands out in my mind. I was releasing a typical Wilma rainbow of about a foot long when a mammoth of three pounds swam right in front of me in two feet of water. By the time I had my gear and my composure in order the fish had moved out of casting range and disappeared. I've also seen many 16-17 inch trout in this little lake, and have caught a number of fine specimens in the 14-15 inch class. The grassy shoreline gives the fish access to swarms of insects, especially terrestrials, and contributes to their quick growth rates. The trout are selective; being right on the Pacific Crest Trail all but guarantees that they will see their share of fish hooks. I found I had to go to a long (14 foot) light (6X) leader before I was consistently hooking fish. It is helpful, almost mandatory, for the angler to wade this lake. Most of the shoreline is marshy, and if you don't get your feet wet you'll be at a great disadvantage.

The biggest rainbows I caught, 15 inches, were tough warriors. They fought exceptionally well—going on sizzling runs into my backing and leaping way out in the middle of the lake. Spotting fish in the shallows, leading them with a soft cast, and then seeing the strike makes for exciting trout fishing at its finest.

The fish eat tiny midges, adults and nymphs, by the hundreds. Caddisflies also work well in sizes 12-16, with the larger sizes matching an olive caddis that emerges in mid-summer. In addition to these aquatic insects, terrestrial patterns are great ammunition for Wilma Lake trout. The often encountered ants and beetles are imitated well with a #18 Sierra Bug or exact ant and beetle patterns. I saw dozens of fish at this lake lying perpendicular to shore with their noses poked into the weed beds waiting to pounce on a wind-blown morsel. A sample also turned up two large drowned bees in the stomach of a 14 inch rainbow. Only rarely have I seen bees being eaten by trout— maybe that classic old pattern the McGinty would work well here.

A happy spin fisherman I came across landed a nice 14 inch bow at Wilma when he switched from lures to a bubble and a fly. This can be a great way for a spin fisherman to fish the surface if trout are rising. The clear casting bubble is placed two to four feet from the fly. Upon impact, if the water is calm, the bubble will scare fish. But, if the fisherman is patient, the fish will resume feeding in a few minutes. On a choppy surface the casting bubble may not disturb the trout at all, and the fisherman may get an immediate strike. In either case it is best to cast the bubble at a bit of a distance from the rising trout and wait for them to swim over and find the fly. The fisherman should strike quickly as the trout are unlikely to hook themselves.

To the north of Wilma Lake is big, long Tilden Lake. From the P.C.T. the Tilden Lake Trail reaches the lake in an uphill mile and a half. The lake itself is about two miles long. If you judge it by its outlet stream and its south end, you'd think it was barren and perhaps pass it by without wetting a line. This would be a mistake for the huge lake is home to hefty rainbow trout. The rainbows, which often reach 17 inches, were stocked in 1911 and again in 1913. These are hot fish that fight and leap and feel much bigger on the line than they end up being in the net. Small mayflies and caddisflies take trout when fish are seen rising mornings and evenings. Spinning gear also seems to work well during midday in this deep lake. The fish regularly feed on flies too small to imitate—tiny size 28 black midges and even smaller green leaf hoppers.

Most trout caught will be pure rainbows, but some will have a little golden trout coloring. Goldens have worked down the creek and have hybridized with some of Tilden's rainbows. I took one 14 inch trout that had a wide red stripe like a rainbow, but the golden yellow belly characteristic of a golden trout—a unique and attractive fish.

This pretty lake is popular with backpackers despite being just off the P.C.T. Still, it is so big it doesn't seem that it could ever get crowded. If you visit it during the middle of the week, early or late in the season, you may very well have it to yourself. Non-backpackers have a hard time imagining a classic alpine lake like Tilden that isn't always overrun with campers and fishermen.

Above Tilden Lake, Tilden Creek provides fishing for small rainbows. Following the creek upstream you'll find rainbow trout that

Tilden Creek. This meadow is about the dividing line between rainbows and pure goldens—a gorgeous uncrowded spot perfect for a picnic lunch.

Author with a golden trout from Tilden Creek.

have hybridized with golden trout to create offspring that display every color of the rainbow. Further upstream the trout are of a pure golden strain. These stunning fish rarely exceed seven inches in this tiny creek. They moved into the creek after being planted in Mary Lake, which lies above. Mary was planted with rainbows in 1911 and 1913, but the early rainbow plants didn't survive. This prompted plantings of goldens in 1935, 1954, and 1964. Most of the planted goldens now live in the creek below the lake, but a few big goldens still await the patient fisherman in the lake. Not many people reach Mary Lake, so the goldens aren't accustomed to seeing fishermen. This doesn't mean they are easy to catch though. The water is clear and there isn't much cover to hide the angler. Light lines and small flies seem to work best. The goldens in the lake average about 12 inches, and some reach 16. In the creek the fish run smaller but hit dry flies with abandon. Goldens have been reported in the 18-20 inch range, but most of those were caught years ago and are extremely rare today. Still, the prospect of catching a 12-16 inch golden is irresistible to many fishermen, myself included.

Some people even go so far as to become specialized golden trout fishermen at the exclusion of all other trout. This may be a worthy aspiration, but it takes a lot of time in addition to a great deal of stamina and perseverance to reach remote, stark golden trout country. Only hardy, determined individuals should consider the sport of looking for high Sierra gold.

A scenic Dorothy Lake as seen from Dorothy Lake Pass.

The P.C.T. follows Falls Creek for many miles as it heads north out of Yosemite. The delightful creek at nearly a 9,000 foot elevation harbors colorful little rainbows that were planted in 1905 and 1913. A few big rainbows (12-14 inches) are found in the creek above Wilma Lake, but most are in the 6-8 inch range. Some sections are swarming with them, while others contain only the odd trout. The Grace Meadow section of Falls Creek is an excellent place to fish dry flies on quiet water for small, but numerous, fish. This is a gorgeous mile-long meadow that reminds me of Tuolumne Meadows without the people. On my last trip through Grace Meadow the only living things I saw besides trout were deer and a golden eagle. I'd heard that there were some big rainbows in this section, but I caught bigger ones both above and below the meadow. Occasionally you may see a rainbow of 10 or 11 inches, although you shouldn't plan on getting a stringer full of them. Mayfly patterns in small sizes work well in the meadow stretches. Size 14-18 flies such as Adams, Mosquitos, and Hendricksons can all be effective, as are terrestrial patterns of beetles, ants, and sometimes grasshoppers. Upper Falls Creek is a classic trout stream in an unbeatable setting—definitely a quality fishing experience.

The P.C.T. leaves Yosemite after skirting the shore of Dorothy Lake and climbing over Dorothy Lake Pass. Dorothy was planted with rainbows in 1911 and 1913, and now claims a substantial population of reproducing trout. The lake is visited on a regular basis all summer, so the fish aren't gullible. The trout strike dry flies during the day, but, of course, mornings and evenings play host to the most surface activity. Tiny black midges and big black caddisflies were the insects most commonly seen in flight when I was staying there. The fish were also eating large (#12) white bodied caddis larvae—case and all. The south end of the lake has large numbers of small trout, while the north end features rainbows that average 13 inches but aren't as plentiful. Dorothy holds a generous supply of 12-14 inch rainbows, and 18 inchers are not unheard of. Thus, Dorothy Lake is a noteworthy "Welcome to Yosemite Trout Fishing" lake for those heading south on the P.C.T. Much fine fishing also awaits Yosemite visitors a few miles down the trail. The same holds true for hikers leaving Yosemite heading north. Between the Yosemite National Park boundary and Sonora Pass you will find many trout-filled lakes and streams waiting to be explored.

Hetch Hetchy Northwestern Backcountry

The area covered in this chapter extends from Hetch Hetchy Reservoir north and west to the national park boundary. The two main trailheads that provide access to this backcountry are found at Hetch Hetchy and at Lake Eleanor. These two lakes can be reached by car, and both offer fine fishing. Hetch Hetchy Reservoir features large rainbow and brown trout. The fishing opportunities in this huge lake are examined in detail in the "Tuolumne River" section of this book. Lake Eleanor also provides good fishing and will be discussed in this section along with the backcountry lakes and streams.

Lake Eleanor is a natural lake that was dammed to raise its level by 35 feet. This was carried out by the city of San Francisco—which was also responsible for building the dam on the Tuolumne River that created Hetch Hetchy Reservoir. The dam at Lake Eleanor was completed in 1918, five years before the O'Shaughnessy Dam at Hetch Hetchy was finished. Eleanor is by far the second biggest body of water in Yosemite (only Hetch Hetchy is bigger). You can drive to the lake from May 1st to September 15th—the road is closed for the winter. You'll find a ranger station at the lake, and you'll also find good rainbow trout fishing. (Be advised: you may also find a rattlesnake or two).

Rainbows were planted in Eleanor in 1877, making it one of the first places in Yosemite that trout were introduced. This, and several other unofficial plants, were performed by pioneer Horace Kibbie who lived in the area. Since this initial plant there have been several others over the years at Lake Eleanor. At some point bluegill and suckers also became established in the lake, so today they are found in addition to rainbow trout.

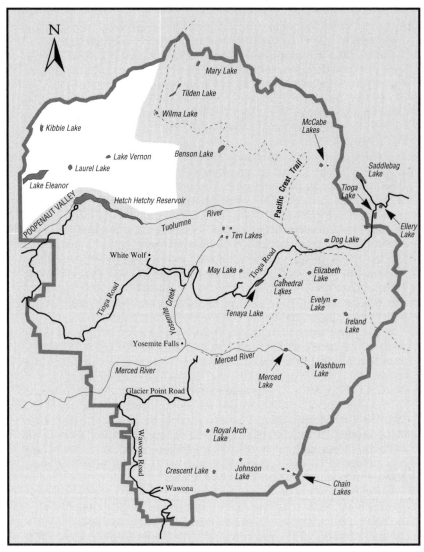

The rainbows are of good size, averaging 12 inches, frequently reaching 16 inches, and sometimes exceeding three pounds. Fish of over five pounds have been reported. Most of the fishing is done with bait or spinning lures, and most of the big fish are taken in this manner. Fly fishermen can enjoy success by using streamer patterns with sinking lines in this big lake. Fish can also be taken on dry flies when they are seen rising on most summer evenings near the inlet and outlet streams. An egg taking station was once located where Frog Creek enters the lake. It was opened in 1933, and has long since closed.

Egg-laden females were stripped, and the eggs were used by the hatchery to plant trout in numerous other Yosemite lakes and streams. Lake Eleanor doesn't get a lot of visitors, so fishing it is never a crowded proposition. Most people who come to the area fish Cherry Lake. Cherry is stocked regularly (it is outside of Yosemite) and has a nice campground and boat ramp. Small rainbows can also be taken from Eleanor and Cherry Creeks below the two dams. Lake Eleanor is also visited by hikers heading into the wilderness.

The story of the backcountry fishing in this region is, unfortunately, largely a tale of past glory. Many lakes that once produced large trout now exist in a fishless state. The decline of this area as a fishery is easily traced to the halting of trout planting in the park. Most of the lakes in the region are not able to support natural reproducing trout populations. The reason for this fact is that the lakes are located at relatively low elevations, and their feeder streams tend to run too low (or dry up completely) to allow ample reproduction for rainbow trout. Some of the lakes still contain trout and seem to have the capability during good water years. Many of these lakes have never held any capacity for reproduction, and relied solely upon regular plantings for their trout populations.

The other contributing factor to the lack of trout in most of these lakes is the choice of trout type that was originally made. The only trout that could survive conditions where feeder streams dry up is the brook trout. Unfortunately, most of these lakes were planted with rainbow trout. Early day planners probably never considered that there would be a time when the planting of trout would cease. In 1941 the Park Service decided not to plant any more brook trout with the exception of waters where they previously existed exclusively. In 1971 they discontinued brook trout planting altogether. There are other lakes in Yosemite that would also be barren if they had been planted with rainbows instead of brook trout.

In the following descriptions I'll focus on the spots that still offer good fishing, while touching on a few of yesterday's legends. If a lake or creek isn't mentioned, the reader can assume (fairly safely) that it is fishless, or soon to be. However, in a few instances (such as small unnamed lakes well off the main trails) there may be trout fishing to be had. These are not discussed for a couple of possible reasons. Namely, they may be unknown to the author, or the author doesn't want to snatch the spirit and excitement of discovery away from those adventurous souls who wish to leave the trail in search of their own secret spots. If you are fortunate enough to find such a spot—enjoy it—as I'm sure you will.

Due to the relatively low elevation and correspondingly long growing season, some of the lakes in this region once grew trout of epic proportions. Swamp Lake comes instantly to mind. It was a brook trout lake, probably the best in Yosemite, and it was close enough to reach on a day hike. The brookies in Swamp Lake often went three or four pounds, and some were caught that weighed five and six pounds. It is now fishless. The other good lakes that are now fishless were mostly rainbow fisheries. These include: Flora Lake which contained two foot long rainbows, Inferno Lake and its two pound rainbows, and Miwok Lake which has held rainbows of four and five pounds. Ardeth and Boundary lakes, both of which formerly provided solid action for good-sized rainbows, are now also barren.

An example of a lake that still provides fishing but will probably soon be fishless is Gravel Pit Lake. It was planted with rainbows as recently as 1987. The trout from that plant will be gone soon—either they will die a natural death or they will be caught. Many other lakes were planted with rainbows over the years but are now devoid of fish life. The Otter Lakes, Peninsula Lakes, Bear Lake, Many Island Lake, Spotted Fawn Lake, and Little Bear Lake all sadly fall into this category. A rather dreary picture of present day fishing is painted by all of this. But, fortunately, there are a few lakes in the vicinity that still provide good fishing, and our attention will now shift to them.

Kibbie Lake has had a long standing reputation as a good rainbow trout fishery. It was planted long ago by Horace Kibbie; in 1878 and 1880. The rainbows reproduced on their own for many decades, and additional plants of rainbows weren't made until 1961. The lake was planted in the 1960s to keep up with increased fishing pressure. The last plant was completed in 1972, and the fish are currently doing well on their own. Most of the rainbows are in the 8-12 inch range, but fish of 14-16 inches are sometimes taken. This shallow, large lake is a good early season bet for fly fishermen. May and June see a lot of surface feeding on mayflies and caddisflies by the hungry rainbows. I found that the largest concentration of fish is on the southern, trail side of the lake. This is convenient, as I spent a lot of time walking to the far side of the lake, without benefit of a trail, only to find that there weren't any fish there. Kibbie is reached by trail from Eleanor Lake, and it does entertain a large number of visitors.

Laurel Lake is also a solid rainbow trout lake. It has a fair population of fish in the 10-14 inch range, with a few that reach the two and three pound mark. I saw some of the bigger fish leaping clear of the water as they chased caddis pupae, but only managed to catch rainbows up to 13 inches. These fish are finely colored. The biggest I took was a beautiful red-cheeked rainbow that weighed a solid pound. Most of the trout are found cruising near the weed beds feasting on the abundant insect life. In addition to dark caddisflies, there are thousands of damselflies, innumerable tiny midges, and thick morning hatches of tan size 14 mayflies. Also available to the trout is that well known high-lake pest, the mosquito. The fish take these one after another when they are in the larval stage.

Fly casting at Kibbie Lake.

The trout are selective in Laurel and can be shy. This lake gets visited regularly by hikers, fishermen, and bears. A mother and cub stopped by to try and share my lunch. They needed some strong urging (in the form of flying rocks) to be convinced that I wasn't intent on showing any hospitality by inviting them to join me in my meal. When the lake fishing is slow, you can spend some time catching little rainbows in the outlet creek. These fish reach about nine inches and are fairly plentiful. Laurel Lake is a challenging fishery that can yield rewards in the form of 16-18 inch rainbows to skilled anglers.

Another easily reached lake with a self-sustaining rainbow population is Lake Vernon. Vernon is similar to Kibbie in many respects. It is also large, shallow, and it too harbors rainbows of up to 16 inches. Rainbows were also planted in Vernon in the very early years—1880 was the first. Early summer is the best time to fish it with flies, but trout feed on the surface all through the season at various times. When the weather gets warm the trout will be on top only in the mornings and evenings. During midday the best success is enjoyed by those who let bait sit in the deepest water. Vernon is reached by trail from Hetch Hetchy, and it, like Kibbie Lake, hosts a large number of fishermen.

Falls Creek, one of the best trout streams in the region, runs into and out of Lake Vernon. Rainbows up to about 16 inches can be taken above and below the lake. Above the lake the creek is slow, wide, and deep for the first 3/4 mile. More fish are found in the faster water upstream of this slow section, some which reach 13-14 inches. Below Vernon is ideal rainbow water featuring riffles, runs, and pockets holding some very nice rainbows. From Vernon down to Hetch Hetchy are half a dozen miles of virtually unfished, excellent rainbow water. Some of the best non-lake rainbows in the entire park can be found in this stretch; trout of 14-18 inches. There is no trail, and there may be rattlesnakes, so you'll have to earn your fish. These factors ensure that there will never be much fishing pressure on this fine water. Falls Creek has a good flow to it—especially in the spring—and its plunge over Wapama Falls into Hetch Hetchy can be spectacular.

Lower Branigan Lake can only be reached by hiking cross-country. This keeps the crowds low and the fishing success high. The closest point of entry is Lake Vernon, but it isn't an easy hike even if it is short in miles. This hike has it all. That is, it has all the obstacles you could imagine. It is steep and slow-going on the ridge as you end up backtracking to maneuver around impassable cliffs and gorges. If you elect to hike below the ridge you find mosquito infested marshes slow your progress. It is extremely brushy in parts, then, when you break through the last of the brush it is straight uphill.

I was also surprised by a rattlesnake in this area. My snake bite kit was back at camp because I assumed I was too high for the nasty critters. But, a rock ledge I jumped onto was already occupied, and it was only a split second before that big rattler had it all to himself again. In addition to being the highest elevation rattler I've ever seen (6,700') it was also the biggest. It was about five feet long and as thick as a baseball bat (a big leaguer's not a little league bat). I'd always heard to look out for rattlesnakes below 6,000 feet, and if an occasional one was found a little higher it would be lethargic and not very healthy. I'd hate to meet a healthier looking snake than the one I saw that day. I've now raised my minimum rattlesnake alert elevation to 7,000 feet and hope I never have to raise it again. I've only seen five rattlesnakes in several hundred miles of hiking in Yosemite, but three of them have been near Hetch Hetchy. This proves to me that its reputation for harboring snakes with fangs is well deserved.

Once you finally reach Branigan you won't find it teeming with fish, but they have reproduced well since the last plant in 1963. The other two Branigan Lakes, Middle and Upper, don't contain trout. Branigan rainbows are typical at 10 inches, but two pounders have been caught. The lake doesn't seem to yield large numbers of trout, still there are enough fish present to keep a fisherman interested. I took 12 and 13 inch rainbows and saw a few bigger ones on my only visit to this pretty, secluded lake. Medium sized caddisflies work well (sizes 10-14)—both when feeding fish are observed and when trying to draw them to the surface.

The fish were surprisingly tough to fool at this lake that is rarely visited. I didn't see any evidence of the lake having been fished in a long while (not a single piece of trash or fishing line) and expected the fish to be easy marks. It turned out that I had to carefully stalk them to entice them into striking. Lower Branigan is a very enticing lake that features good rainbow fishing in an unspoiled, serene setting.

From the trail along Falls Creek at lower Jack Main Canyon, an adventurous fisherman can hike cross-country to rainbow filled Edyth and Bearup lakes. Edyth has rainbows in the 10-14 inch range and sees very few fishermen per season. Anyone who makes the difficult trip in should find solitude and willing trout. I believe the rainbows can reproduce well at Edyth and will continue to thrive in this remote lake. Bearup Lake is easier to reach than Edyth and also features good-sized rainbows. It was planted in 1942, and sometimes surrenders rainbows of 14 to 17 inches. Frog Creek is its feeder stream, and smaller rainbows can be taken above and below the lake. Frog Creek was planted with rainbows sometime before 1913—the exact date is unknown.

The above is a rather brief list of the fish-worthy named lakes of the region. There are not many. They are far outnumbered, as you can easily see, by the fishless lakes that exist. I spent some time covering the lakes devoid of fish in order to save the reader a lot of lost time and many wasted steps. However, as I stated earlier, there may be a few lakes that hold trout that are unknown to me and to almost everyone else. One such lake is located somewhere in Jack Main Canyon. Mike Finley, Superintendent of Yosemite National Park, spoke of one that he had found. At a meeting discussing the future of trout fishing in the park, I spoke—informally—to Mr. Finley during a break in the proceedings. He mentioned a small unnamed lake in Jack Main Canyon that contained fat rainbows in the two pound class. He had caught them the previous summer and was looking forward to returning. I don't blame him for not giving away the exact location of this hidden treasure. A small lake like the one he described couldn't stand much fishing pressure before it would become fished out. There may be other little trout-filled lakes that are just spots on the map to all but a select few tight-lipped individuals. The odds are high, however, that most of the lakes in this region, named or unnamed, do not contain trout. But, if you find yourself close to an uncharted piece of water, you may consider taking a look at it—you might find your own personal trout fishing paradise.

The creeks in this region suffer in a manner similar to that of the lakes. The lack of water sometimes dries up the creeks. In an extended drought period the entire trout population of a creek can be wiped out. A moderate drought can nearly wipe out the fish, only to see a few survive in the deeper holes and then repopulate the creek. The dozens of miles of creeks in this region have held trout in varying quantities for nearly a century. The status of these trout populations is ever changing and fluctuates from year to year. The creeks that have the largest consistent water volume are also the ones that probably will have stable trout populations. Frog Creek and Falls Creek are the two best trout fishing creeks in this area. Both hold rainbows, and Falls Creek contains the bigger fish of the two. In Paradise Valley and up through Jack Main Canyon the rainbows in Falls Creek are common in the 10-12 inch range. They do grow larger, and sometimes reach 16 inches. I've caught enough 14 and 15 inch rainbows in this stretch to truly appreciate the fine fishing it provides. Fly fishermen do best in most stretches of the average creek, as many creeks are too small for spinning gear. This holds true for Falls Creek. The deeper holes and pools of Falls Creek are good spots for bait and spinners, and this is where the one pound rainbows are most often found. Almost any small dry fly will draw plenty of strikes from the good population of rainbows in this fine creek.

Frog Creek has a good flow of water to it, and is a delightful place to fish. It's loaded with small rainbows and is a very pretty creek. It's fairly easy to follow (even without a trail running alongside) if you are willing to get in the water and wade your way upstream. This is another spot where a beginning fly fisher could have a great time. You're always fishing over plenty of willing trout, so you're sure to catch some. Nothing beats the experience gained from actually catching fish. You can do all the reading and video watching in the world, but no lesson will be as well learned as that learned afield. As evidence of the quantities of 5-8 inch rainbows that abound in Frog Creek, I once took over 20 of the pesky little bows from a single pool in this gentle creek.

Rainbows are also scattered throughout Miguel, Kibbie, Bartlett, Kendrick, and Eleanor Creeks. Some of these populations wax and wane with the water conditions, and some are replenished by trout migrating from the lakes that they connect.

Kibbie Creek, below the lake, has some real nice rainbows living in its mossy water. They aren't abundant like those found in Frog Creek, but their average size is excellent for a creek. There is usually one good fish in each desirable hole, ranging from 9-14 inches. I took five trout in two hours of fly casting here that averaged a more than respectable 12 inches. These fish were caught on assorted dry flies in sizes 12-14. There was a large, dark, slate winged mayfly hatching in mid-June on my last visit. Once you get a half mile below the lake it's a little tough to bushwhack your way down the lower trailless section, but the lure of plump, strong trout can lead you to the quality uncrowded fishing found in this mileage. Kibbie Creek is a solid early season bet for surprisingly hefty rainbows.

The creeks on the eastern side of this region that provide the best trout fishing are Rancheria Creek and Tiltill Creek. Rancheria has a large volume of water in it and often has sizable rainbows living below its falls. Trout from Hetch Hetchy can move upstream for about a mile to Rancheria Falls, and these rainbows sometimes push 15 inches. There aren't usually a lot of fish in this lower mile, but sometimes the fishing can be noteworthy. Above the falls the trout are not densely populated. They will reach about 10 inches, but are spottily scattered.

The feeder creeks to Rancheria also hold little rainbows in small numbers. These include the seldom visited Deep Canyon Branch, and the easily accessible Tiltill Mountain Branch. The creeks in this area were planted with brook trout in 1905, however I've only caught rainbows. Tiltill Creek also has some small rainbows living in it. Tiltill Valley yeilds rainbows in the 6-10 inch range, but they aren't extremely numerous. Incidentally, don't plan on fishing Tiltill Creek at the trail crossing along Hetch Hetchy Reservoir. At this spot a bridge crosses a deep gorge that makes the creek inaccessible. Most of the miles of Tiltill Creek and Rancheria Creek (and nearly all of the creeks in this region) are very seldom visited. They mostly run away from trails and are difficult to follow. Some may have pockets of abundant trout, but most will be small.

Of all the creeks in the area, an angler couldn't do much better than to spend time on Falls Creek. From Lake Vernon to Wilma Lake, Falls Creek may provide the best stream fishing in the park in certain sections. The fish tend to be concentrated in some parts of the creek and absent in others. If you find one of the well populated sections you can enjoy first rate rainbow fishing in a creek that has it all. Namely, it's pretty, uncrowded, big enough for enjoyable fly casting, and not too big so as to be intimidating. It offers all water types from deep pools and runs to shallow riffles and pockets. This stretch also has the added bonus of being above the rattlesnakes and poison oak. And finally, it contains superb sized rainbows that often reach 16 inches. Falls Creek would be my clear number one choice for fishing moving water in the northwestern backcountry.

Many other area creeks offer solitude; if somewhat uncertain, inconsistent fishing. I wouldn't recommend heading a long way off the trail with one of these other creeks as my destination. However, I always check a creek that I cross when heading cross-country to a lake. Also, if trout are found in a creek, it can often be productive to follow it away from trails where the fish may be more numerous and more sizeable.

Wawona—South Boundary

Wawona sits at the southern end of Yosemite on the banks of the South Fork of the Merced River. The historic Wawona Hotel is the centerpiece of the area as it sits overlooking the Wawona Golf Course

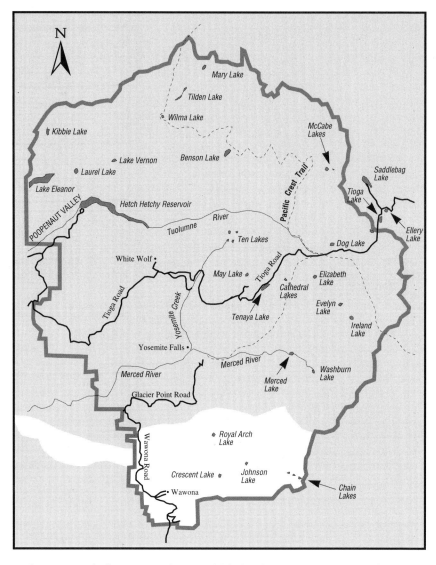

(nine very challenging and scenic holes). The Mariposa Grove of giant sequoias is nearby. Fishing is not the number one activity in the area, but that's not to say there aren't good fishing opportunities present. Most of the fishing is done in the South Fork itself, but there are several feeder streams that also contain trout. There are no lakes in this vicinity that can be reached by either automobile or by an easy day hike. All the lakes in the south boundary area require at least an overnight trip in order to be fished properly. There are some good fish to be had in many of these lakes, and they will be covered later in this chapter. Any discussion of the fishing around Wawona should start with the South Fork of the Merced. It is the only river in the area, and as it makes its way downstream it is joined by many feeder streams that increase its volume. There is road access to a few miles of the river and a fine campground is located on its banks. The stretch near the campground and along the highway is not the best place to fish as it gets hit mighty hard by thousands of tourists each summer. But, fish can be caught here. The best tactic to use to increase your odds is simply to cross the river and fish the opposite bank. The best spots I've found are the points where feeder streams enter the river. Near the campground these are Big Creek and Rush Creek.

The trout in this part of the river are almost all rainbows under a foot long. These fish are natives or ancestors of formerly stocked trout. There are a few browns caught here, and some of them are quite substantial. It seems that every year a few 3-5 pounders are landed, causing a commotion among the local fishing community.

Dry flies work well in the size 12-16 range, matching the small mayflies and caddisflies that hatch most of the summer. There is a good population of stonefly nymphs in this section, so a size six brown stonefly nymph pattern is an excellent choice if there is no hatch. The fish near the campground are accustomed to seeing worms, salmon eggs, and power bait, so other methods are usually more effective.

Heading upstream the fish are more plentiful and less selective. You can follow the river upstream on a side road for a mile or so, and then continue to follow it on a foot trail. The further you get from the road and campground, the better your chances get for catching rainbow trout. There are no browns above the junction with Chilnualna Creek. If you venture further upstream near the headwaters you will find brook trout joining the rainbows. Brookies were first planted in the 1890s in the upper South Fork, and they have done well. Cutthroat trout were planted in 1893, but soon died out—cutthroat have never done well in Yosemite despite many attempts at establishing them in a variety of locations. Downstream near Wawona browns were planted many times between 1923 and 1944. Browns were never planted in the upper section and none are found here. The water above Wawona is best suited for rainbows; it is shallow, swift, and rocky. This is ideal water for the wading fly fisherman.

Downstream from the Wawona Campground the South Fork leaves the road and flows through a wild canyon on its way to join the main Merced River at Savage's Trading Post on Highway 140. This twenty mile stretch of river can only be reached by foot. You can hike downstream for a short distance along the river on a fisherman's trail across from the campground. Another trail, the Alder Creek Trail,

A buck seen near Wawona.

takes you to the river near where Bishop Creek comes in. This is a steep four and a half mile hike that leads to a section of the South Fork that has a good population of brown trout. The browns are outnumbered about four to one by the rainbows, but they will be bigger. You can follow the river downstream via the Alder Creek Trail that will take you to the confluence with the main Merced. It's a good trail that follows the north side of the river most of the way. However, it does cross the river twice, and there are currently no bridges or cables across the water. During high water the river can't be forded at these places.

There is another way to reach the middle part of the roadless section of the South Fork. Roads (paved and dirt) from the Mariposa-Midpines area will get you to the top of the river canyon at Snyder Gulch. From there you hike, making a very steep descent into the river canyon. This is the way I took on my only extensive backpack trip to this area. My goal was to reach the rumored fine fishing near Peach Tree Bar. The information that I had was sketchy and years old, but the promise of 12-16 inch rainbows was enough to tempt me. I found the fishing to be poor and the water (in mid-June) to be very warm. Only a few small trout were hooked by myself and my companion, and only a few more were even seen. There is no possible way that the area could have been suffering from fishing pressure. I blame the extended drought for the high water temperatures and lack of trout (my fishing companion, Matt Burtch, blamed me). We didn't see any other people, nor did we see signs of previous fishermen—no worm cans, broken line, salmon egg jars, or litter of any kind. This is a wild area and a rugged canyon. If the trout population ever recovers it would be a classic place to fish. The water is beautiful with deep pools, long riffles and runs, and plenty of rapids and pocket water. I found a fair amount of caddis and mayfly nymphs, and each night there were good hatches of both. The only problem, and not a minor one to a fisherman, was that there weren't any fish rising to the hatch. I saw one trout of about 16 inches in a deep run, but that was the only fish of any size seen in two full days on the river.

This canyon is a wintering ground for the Yosemite deer herd, and there are known to be plenty of mountain lions that follow them in. I also saw the skeleton of a black bear right on the trail, the only time I'd seen a bear that wasn't alive.

The trout in this middle section are all browns as far as I could tell, although we didn't catch enough for a true sampling. I would guess that the water is too warm for rainbows, and the fine rainbow fishing of years past is no longer found this far downstream. This roadless area of the South Fork cannot be recommended for its fishing, but its rugged isolated character make for a fine wilderness experience.

The lowest portion of river is best reached from its confluence with the main Merced. Access here is achieved by following the popular trail upstream toward Hite Cove. The trailhead is well marked on Highway 140, and is used mostly by early season hikers looking for colorful wildflowers. Some good browns have been seen in the deep holes along this lower few miles of river, but there are more smallmouth bass and trash fish found here than trout.

Some tributaries to the South Fork offer as good or even better fishing than the river itself. Upstream in the headwaters most of the feeder creeks hold small trout. Crescent Creek has brookies, Givens Creek holds rainbows, and Johnson Creek has both. These creeks, along with the upper South Fork, are loaded with trout and don't receive much fishing attention.

Near Wawona, Chilnualna Creek offers enjoyable fishing for rainbows and brookies that were both planted in 1892. Fishing here is done in pretty surroundings with the added bonus of seeing Chilnualna Falls if you hike far enough upstream. This makes for a nice combination sightseeing/fishing day hike. Above the falls all the way to the Chilnualna Lakes, the creek provides classic trout fishing. The only drawback is that the fish are on the small side—averaging eight inches and seldom exceeding 10. However, the best holes (which are spaced far apart) do contain a smattering of 10-13 inch trout, the biggest being rainbows. The creek is very attractive, and a perfect size for the wading fisherman to enjoy following its course upstream while plucking colorful, frisky trout from every step pool. I've taken rainbows to 12 inches and brookies to 11 inches on various dry flies in this ideal dry fly creek. Most of the creek remains virtually unfished year after year, especially the stretches that flow away from the trail. It is one of my favorite Yosemite creeks, so I'm glad it's underfished.

I met a couple of Europeans who saw me fishing it one fine summer day. They told me it was beautiful and then asked where all the people were. They had come from the crowded Yosemite Valley and were glad to get away from the hordes of people, but were surprised at how easy it was to escape them. They assured me that in Europe there was nowhere you could hike only a few miles to a beautiful spot and find solitude. I also had a humorous exchange with them trying to explain the concept of catch and release fishing—which I don't believe they ever quite grasped. Our discussion went something like this:

European: "You catch fish?"

Me: "Yes, I've caught a few."

European (nodding): "So you not have to carry food."

Me: "No, I still carry food, I let the fish go."

European (puzzled): "Why you fish then?"

Me: "For fun."

European (more puzzled): "I don't understand."

Me: "Like a sport."

European (smiling): "Oh, see if you can beat fish?"

Me: "Yes, something like that."

European (feigning understanding): "Oh."

I was probably the subject of a few stories when they returned home. "Remember that whacky American who was catching fish and then letting them go. . ."

Big Creek also empties into the South Fork near Wawona. Its upper reaches can be found by taking good dirt roads out of Fish Camp just south of the National Park boundary. Big Creek doesn't live up to its name, but it does have a decent head of water. It was planted regularly with rainbows in the first half of the century. The lower portion has a large population of willing rainbows in its rock-strewn course, though they aren't very big. The average fish is about eight inches, with an occasional one in the 10-12 inch range. Browns are found further upstream above Laurel Creek (which has brook trout). The browns were planted in 1944 and have done well after that one time planting. I haven't seen any real big ones, (I've caught a few in the 12-16 inch range), but this creek used to have a reputation as a good big brown trout fishery. Perhaps there are some lunker browns upstream in the deeper holes waiting for patient evening bait fishermen. I've had equal success using size 14 Hare's Ear Nymphs and various dries in the same size. As in many creeks, the fish aren't too particular about what flies they take as long as they haven't been alarmed by a careless approach. Big Creek sees more fishermen than any of the other tributaries to the South Fork, but still has plenty of trout to go around.

Big Creek in its full glory thanks to the heavy late spring run-off.

Further north of Wawona Highway 41 crosses Alder and Bishop Creeks, both of which hold trout. Both can be followed upstream into the mountains or downstream toward the South Merced. Locals caution against following the downstream stretches of either, as rattlesnakes are often encountered. A mixture of browns and rainbows are found in the lower mile of each. Alder Creek is the better of the two creeks, featuring more and bigger trout, along with a spectacular, relatively unknown, waterfall. Bishop is small, brushy, and difficult to fish. Browns were planted in Alder Creek first in 1897, and in Bishop in 1931 and 1933. Brook trout were planted in Alder for the first time in 1891, and in Bishop in 1905. An occasional brook trout is taken in the upper reaches of these creeks, but in general, browns and rainbows dominate. A good bet for ambitious hikers is to fish these creeks at their confluence with the South Merced. Fish taken there are generally larger than those found upstream, which seldom top 10 inches.

The south boundary country offers good lake fishing for the backpacking fisherman. The fishing is generally good, and is often very good, in many of these lakes for some nice trout. Prospecting the inlet and outlet streams can be fun—although the fish will generally be smaller than those found in the lakes. It is best to visit these lakes early in the season when the trails first become free of snow. At this time the bugs are getting active, the fish are hungry, and other fishermen haven't appeared yet. The summer fishing is usually slower except for brief periods: mornings and evenings. Fishing picks up again later in the season, with September and October being excellent times. In fall the water is cooler and the fish are on the prowl trying to fatten up before the long winter. In brook trout waters fall is an exceptional time to fish because they will be spawning. They'll be very active and extremely colorful. A spawning male brook trout is perhaps the most spectacular looking of all trout. The lakes in this section of Yosemite are all rather small (under 30 acres) but there are fish to be caught up to 15 inches.

Leaving South Wawona on the Chilnualna Creek Trail, then heading east toward Buck Camp, brings you first to fishless Grouse Lake, then to fishless Crescent Lake. Johnson Lake is found along the trail in another mile. If you didn't know better you'd think Johnson Lake was also fishless as it looks like the other two lakes, shallow and weedy. My brother and I made this mistake and passed it by the first time we visited this area. However, it has a fairly good population of rainbows. In the past Johnson has had rainbows, brooks, and browns living in it, but now only the rainbows remain. This lake does get some fishing pressure, so the fish can be difficult to fool. They average about 10 inches, with plenty of 12 inchers, and a few reaching 14-15 inches. Small flies worked near the weed beds are a good bet.

There are rainbows in Johnson Creek (also a few brookies), but in low water years they are cut off from the lake. The first half mile above the lake is slow and clear giving fish and fisherman a chance to see each other. There are some nice fish here—rainbows of 10-14 inches, but they require the stealth of a hunter to approach. I managed to hook the biggest fish I saw in this stretch, a fine 14 inch rainbow, but we parted company after he quickly wrapped my line around a couple of logs. The problem presented here is that the tippets required to fool these fish aren't very strong, so once hooked the trout has a definite advantage over the angler. This makes for a challenge that can be a lot of fun.

Royal Arch Lake is nearby, and is a fine place for a layover day for the traveling fisherman. It's a very pretty, small, deep lake. Royal Arch holds mostly brook trout with a few rainbows sometimes caught. The lake was first planted with brookies in 1897 and last planted with this species in 1934. Brook trout do much better than rainbows here, and probably will totally replace them in time. On my last visit I caught 30 fish—all were brook trout between eight and 12 inches. Some trout reach 14 inches in this deep lake. On my first trip here, my brother and I didn't catch any of the bigger fellas, but we saw them swimming just out of casting range. Bill didn't try too hard though. A long drive to the trailhead, then the taxing hike in had him more interested in napping and swimming than in fishing. So, my flies outfished his spinners in an unfair test. Browns were planted in Royal Arch in 1930 but haven't been caught since the 1970s. If you're looking for a pretty lake that's loaded with trout and isn't too hard to reach, Royal Arch would be hard to beat. It is a popular lake with backpackers so fishing success is greater for those who go early and late in the season.

Further east is Givens Lake, which requires a short cross-country hike to reach. The lake no longer has rainbows as they don't seem able to reproduce in this shallow warm lake. They were planted many times without long term success until 1969, but the 1934 plant of brook trout has survived. There are some good brook trout in Givens, a few reaching 15 inches. There aren't many fish in the lake but the ones caught will be of good size. Small caddisflies live in the lake and hatch on summer afternoons and evenings. Dragonfly and damselfly nymphs also populate this lake, so the fly fisherman can cast imitations of these during the morning and midday hours. Size 14 Elk Hair Caddis patterns work well when fish are rising.

At the extreme southeastern corner of Yosemite lie some fertile trout lakes. The three Chain Lakes all offer good fishing. The easiest way to reach these lakes is to hike in from the south by way of Chiquito Pass (this pass is sometimes referred to as Chiquita—even on some of the trail signs in Yosemite—but the sign at the actual pass says Chiquito, as does the official map of the park). The trailhead is reached from outside Yosemite on roads originating from the town of Oakhurst. The trail leads to the lowest lake and reaches all three lakes: Lower Chain, Middle Chain, and Upper Chain.

The Chain Lakes can be excellent for chunky rainbow and brook trout; some weighing over a pound. However, they tend to be crowded all summer and heavily fished. The time to hit these lakes is very early in the season before the crowds come and catch the best fish—or scare them into the depths. The angler willing to haul a float tube up here would most likely be rewarded with an increased catch—the same holds true for almost all backcountry lakes.

Lower Chain has rainbows up to 14 inches. The average size is about nine inches, and there is a good population of foot long fish, with just enough bigger fish to liven up the proceedings. Mayflies, caddisflies, and midges are all present in this lake. I've found that small dark midge dry flies (18-22) work well even in the middle of the season, as do small, dependable ant patterns. The fish generally see larger lures and baits, but won't shy away from such tiny flies. This shallow yet productive lake features, like all three of these lakes, classic alpine beauty.

The creek below Lower Chain has small rainbows and brookies in each of its bigger rocky pockets and plunge pools all the way down to where it joins the South Fork of the Merced near Soda Springs. The creek between Lower and Middle Chain is full of bigger rainbows in the 8-11 inch range—a decent size for a small creek. Hint: Don't pass up the marshy ponds that get isolated from the grassy creek during the late summer and fall. Trout get trapped in these as they wait for more water to come down the creek and reopen their access to the creek and lake. I took a few of the hardest hitting 10 inch rainbows I've seen from these ponds. The fish are hungry and not shy. I watched a 10 inch trout gobble down a three inch dragonfly just a few feet in front of me. I've rarely seen a trout eat an adult dragonfly, and I wasn't expecting the relatively small trout to capture such a feast.

Middle Chain has mostly rainbows living in its deep waters, but brook trout do come down from the upper lake on occasion. The trout population isn't as dense here as at either of the other two lakes in the chain, but this is where the biggest fish are found. The average size of these colorful trout is an impressive 11 inches. On a sparkling first day of fall, on my first visit to these lakes, I was pleased to take a trio of sporty 13 inch rainbows on dry flies while I saw a few 15 inch bruisers that I couldn't entice. This is the most heavily fished of the three lakes, so the fish aren't easy. I got many refusals here, and at Lower Chain, where fish would nose my fly after I thought I'd made the perfect leading cast to the shoreline cruisers. As usual, my success rate increased in direct proportion to the size of my fly, with the smaller flies getting less refusals and drawing more impetuous strikes.

Upper Chain is the least visited, least fished, and most scenic of the three lakes. It contains the most trout that also are the easiest to catch. The only drawback is that the trout are smaller than at the other lakes. There are no rainbows in Upper Chain, only brook trout. It is loaded with 8-10 inch ravenous, colorful brookies. There are a few (very few) 11-12 inch trout, but for the most part they are pan sized. The creek below the lake is also full of small brookies. The rainbows from the lower lakes can't get upstream very far because of cascades and small waterfalls, but the brook trout do go downstream from time to time in search of water with less competition. It's possible to catch brook trout on almost every cast at Upper Chain, but if you're looking for bigger fish you're better off at the lower lakes. This is a great lake for kids or for beginners who just want to catch some wild trout, regardless of size. Even an advanced fisherman can have fun at Upper Chain. It's a good place to go for the ego—especially if you're getting shut out at the lower lakes. The magnificent scenery, high quality fishing, and relatively easy hike in, make for a winning combination at all of the Chain Lakes.

From Upper Chain Lake it is a short, but steep cross-country hike to Breeze Lake. The ducked route to Breeze takes about a half hour as it climbs the near 10,000 foot ridge that separates it from Upper Chain. There once was a fair population of rainbows reaching about a foot in length, but unfortunately I found this stunningly beautiful lake to be fishless. I casted for an hour while circling it, and saw no fish— nor did I see any rises anywhere on the calm surface. Like other lakes in the area, Breeze was planted with brown trout long ago, but there is no evidence of them today. It was planted with rainbows as recently as 1969, and the 1977 study done by the Park Service found those fish to be reproducing at a moderate level. It is possible that there are a few rainbows left in the lake (maybe big ones if they have it to themselves), but I presume that the small population was wiped out forever by the extended drought. I hope I'm wrong, as it would be a shame for this deep blue, peak-encircled lake to be barren. I only include it here because someone may want to take a chance that it still holds rainbows, they may just want to visit it for the scenery, or I may save someone the difficult scramble required to reach it if they know it probably is fishless.

The only lake worth trying to the north over Merced Pass is Lower Ottoway Lake. The two Merced Pass Lakes used to have a reputation for great rainbow fishing. Unfortunately, rainbows can't reproduce in these lakes, so after the last plant in 1972 they were destined to die out. This ended a long term of fine fishing. This happened naturally enough in the upper lake, but the process was sped up unnaturally and strangely in the lower lake. A small plane crashed into Lower Merced Pass Lake in 1976. The petroleum and other chemicals that leaked from the plane apparently killed all the remaining trout.

Upper Ottoway Lake was also known as a good rainbow lake featuring fat two pound fish. However, the rainbows couldn't reproduce and the lake is now fishless. Lower Ottoway does have a reproducing population of rainbows. It isn't teeming with trout, but some do reach the 12-16 inch range. Ottoway Creek also affords some good fishing for somewhat smaller rainbow trout.

If you were to stay to the north following Chilnualna Creek from Wawona, you would come to the Chilnualna Lakes. The trail leads first to the lower lake that is fishless, and then to the upper lake that is loaded with brookies that reach 11 inches. I fished it just after ice out one year and caught fish one after the other until I was tired of it. The trail still had snow on it in many places so I doubt that many parties had reached the lake before me. I was literally able to catch a brook trout on every cast. Later in the season the fishing naturally slows down, but this is still a solid lake for medium sized brook trout. The middle lake is reached by a short cross-country hike and holds slightly larger brook trout in similar quantities and sizes as the upper lake, but has the added advantage of being less crowded.

Continuing up the Buena Vista Trail takes the hiker to picturesque Buena Vista Lake. Now a brook trout lake, Buena Vista is another lake that once was known for providing good rainbow fishing. The brook trout do very well, having maintained themselves for over 70 years since the last stocking (1921). The lake isn't loaded with fish, but some of them do get a foot long—an ample size for brookies. Below the lake, and all along the Buena Vista Trail, Buena Vista

Creek offers fair fishing for rainbow and brook trout. The rainbows are survivors from earlier unsuccessful plants in the lake. Nearby Hoover Creek also has both types of trout that seldom exceed eight inches. A tough cross-country hike will get you to the three Hoover Lakes. Only the western lake has good fishing for a small population of ample sized brookies. Some of these brookies have been reported up to 14 inches. Very few people make the tough hike to this lake, but those who do may find some big brookies waiting for them.

Tuolumne River

The Tuolumne is the 'other' river of Yosemite National Park. Since it doesn't run through the popular and populated Yosemite Valley, it isn't as well known as the Merced River, but it is just as spectacular. Its headwaters are in the high peaks on the eastern side of the park, and the river runs from east to west all the way across Yosemite. It changes character during this journey, and affords the angler all types of fishing opportunities.

The Tuolumne is most famous, or infamous, for the dam that blocks its course. The O'Shaughnessy Dam forms the Hetch Hetchy Reservoir on the western side of the park. This, the only river dam inside the park, was tremendously controversial from the time it was initially proposed until its completion in 1923. John Muir and part of the Sierra Club waged a long battle against the dam, claiming that the now flooded Hetch Hetchy Valley was similar to Yosemite Valley— and therefore was too valuable a treasure to be lost. The Sierra Club itself was split over this issue. My wife's great, great grandfather, Warren Olney Sr., a San Francisco lawyer, was one of the original founders of the Sierra Club. He was the club's first vice-president while Muir was the first president. He was in favor of the dam as a necessary water source for San Francisco, and Hetch Hetchy was seen as a convenient location for a dam. His son, Warren Olney Jr., also an original member of the club, sided with Muir on this issue. Needless to say, this was a sensitive subject at family gatherings. While it is true that San Francisco needed a reservoir for a water source, I wish that the dam could have been built somewhere downstream out of the national park in a less scenic spot.

Hetch Hetchy Valley used to be fine fishing grounds for hefty native rainbow trout. Now, the reservoir is known to be home to some very large rainbow and brown trout, many from 15 to 20 inches in length. These fish can be hard to reach though. No fishing from boats is allowed, and many fish stay deep. Some excellent fish are taken by bank fishermen, mostly with spinning lures and bait. Like any large lake (and it is large—7 miles long and 1/2 mile wide) it is best fished early and late in the day, and early and late in the season.

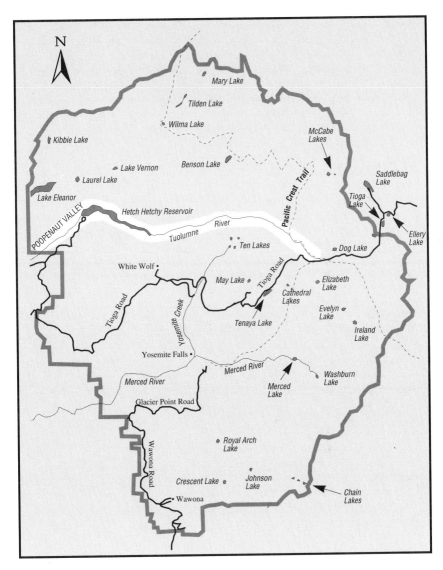

Ambitious fishermen probably could take some big trout by fishing above the lake late in the season for fall spawning browns. This requires a long tough hike to the far side of the lake where the river enters.

The water below the dam is also home to some very big trout. Here, in Poopenaut Valley, large pools and deep runs hold both rainbows and browns. This stretch of water runs from the dam to the western boundary of the park. The biggest fish are browns, and again the problem is in getting to them. First of all, the hike in is straight downhill and is probably the steepest trail I've ever been down. Make sure and check the brakes on your legs before you go. The next problem is in trying to follow the river to fish it. When you get down to the water it's extremely rough going along the banks both above and below Poopenaut Valley. The water in the valley itself is generally shallow and holds few fish. This is unfortunate because the valley is the only place where it is easy to follow the course of the river with anything approaching ease. There are no trails along the river upstream or down, so the fisherman must scramble over rocks and through brush to get from pool to pool. It's too deep to wade in most places, and doesn't readily lend itself to fly fishing. Many spots are more suitable for bait fishing or spin fishing with heavy lures. Bears are found in the area, and there's also poison oak along the banks of the river.

If you aren't discouraged yet, there is also the rattlesnake factor. Rattlers are found scattered all over the west, but the area around Hetch Hetchy has long been known for having an unusually large population of buzztails. They aren't really anything to fear, unless you step on one, (though I fear them far more than black bears) their presence is cause for concern. Since fishing this part of the river involves a good deal of climbing and clambering over rocks, anyone fishing this stretch should be alert. Last spring I saw a few snakes here, but only one I could identify as a rattler.

An old-timer once told me of his remedy for the snake problem on the Tuolumne. He said he and his fishing buddies (when they were young and fit enough to go into Poopenaut Valley) would fashion tin leggings running from their boots to their knees. A rattler striking anyone in this party would be in for quite a surprise.

Another source for rattlesnake information on the Tuolumne River in this area is John Muir himself. In one of the rare times he wasn't writing euphorically and ecstatically about Yosemite, Muir describes being bothered by rattlers as he made his way along the Tuolumne Canyon. In his journals (published after his death) he wrote about his 1895 trip. He made the following references to rattlesnakes: "I saw two rattlesnakes today." "...I came suddenly upon another big rattler this morning; my foot was within five inches of his head ere I discovered him and bounced back." "I met a rattlesnake while scrambling near the river..." "I decided to camp on top of a large boulder a snake could not climb..." The snake situation has changed little in the 100 years since Muir's trip.

If you're still brave enough to fish this area, you may be rewarded with some good fish. I caught a few small rainbows and a couple of chunky, finely marked browns around two pounds last spring. I also hooked and subsequently lost a brown of about 18 inches and three pounds. I was casting, clinging to a tree with one arm, on a rock cliff

40 feet above the water. I'm not sure how I would have landed the fish from that position, so it's probably just as well that he threw the hook early in our battle. I saw other fish in this size range rising for dry flies. An occasional monster of two feet or more is sometimes spotted in this part of the river. Not all the big fish are trout however, as the river does hold some Sacramento suckers.

The best flies for this deep water are large stonefly nymph imitations and large streamers that enable you to get down to the fish. When trout are seen rising chances are that they are taking caddisflies in the size 12-16 range, or else tiny midges. The two best fish I've caught here were on a size 18 gray midge dry, and a size 20 Pheasant Tail Nymph. A small mayfly (*Baetis*) also hatches here, and is imitated well with a size 16 or 18 Adams or mosquito pattern. I'd want tan and olive bodied Elk Hair Caddis dry flies in sizes 12-16 for morning and evening hatches. During midday, when no risers are seen, caddis pupal patterns and Gold Ribbed Hare's Ears in these same sizes and colors can be effective.

Most of the trout caught are of good size and these hard-to-reach fish are bigger than those in any other part of the Tuolumne inside the park. The water stays at a constant temperature below the dam, creating a good habitat for trout even on the warmest summer days. Only about one fisherman per day fishes this beautiful valley, due to its ruggedness, so it will never be fished out. On the hike out you will find Poopenaut Valley aptly named (you will probably be 'poopen' out'). It is 1,000 feet straight up, and it's best not to make the hike during the heat of midday.

Above Hetch Hetchy Reservoir, the Tuolumne becomes an unchecked wild river all the way to its source. The stretch of river from the reservoir upstream to the falls is the wildest and least visited portion. This is the Grand Canyon of the Tuolumne. It requires a full day's hike each way to reach. So, when fishing here, three days is the minimum amount of time you should allow for the trip. Pate Valley is a popular camping spot (for backpackers and for bears), but above Pate Valley the river canyon sees few visitors.

There is a good trail that runs along the river all the way to Tuolumne Meadows, some 25 miles upstream. A person hiking this trail can imagine the difficulty John Muir had fighting his way up the river canyon without benefit of a trail while becoming the first person to successfully accomplish the feat. If you come here to fish, you will be fishing in the river exclusively. There are no lakes nearby, and few feeder streams that carry much water on a year-round basis. If you seek uncrowded fishing on a beautiful river this is a good place to find it. The fishing action is solid, but rarely great. The biggest fish will be in the lower reaches above Hetch Hetchy. Some big fish make their spawning runs out of the reservoir and up the Tuolumne—rainbows in the spring, and browns in the fall. These

Fly casting in Tuolumne Meadows during mid-summer.

are the times when the fishing can be exciting as large trout become more likely targets.

The resident fish that live year-round in the river are also browns and rainbows. The rainbow was the only native trout below the cascades, while the brown was introduced in the first part of the century, starting in 1920. There are some good-sized browns lurking about in the holes, but not as many as you might hope for. Most of the trout caught will be under a pound. These are all wild fish that are unfamiliar with humans. As long as the angler keeps himself out of sight and keeps his shadow off the water, he should find success with any number of lures, baits, or flies. A grasshopper, live or imitation, is a must for the area around Pate Valley. Further upstream there will be more brook trout (first planted in 1906) and fewer rainbows. Browns are found the entire length of the river. Small dry flies imitating mayflies and caddisflies are effective when the fish are rising. There are many pools and deep holes that are best fished with spinning gear. The fly fisherman would be well advised to have sinking line and some big streamers for these holes.

Upstream of the Grand Canyon of the Tuolumne you enter an amazing stretch of river. Most people reach this area by hiking downstream from Tuolumne Meadows. In the meadows the river is smooth and quiet, but downstream it takes on a much different character, dropping quickly in elevation for the next several miles after leaving the meadows. Tuolumne Meadows down to Waterwheel Falls (a distance of about 10 miles) is perhaps the most spectacular stretch of river I have ever seen—especially during the run-off period. The river seems angry and impatient as it makes a series of incredible leaps over waterfalls and down cascades. First comes Tuolumne Falls, then White Cascade—at the bottom of which sits Glen Aulin High Sierra Camp. Next comes the multi-tiered California Falls, followed by LeConte Falls, and finally the sensational Waterwheel Falls. All this within 10 miles of Tuolumne Meadows! An energetic hiker could see all these falls and return to Tuolumne Meadows in one day. Besides the named falls there are other rapids and cascades of tremendous beauty and power. The Pacific Crest Trail follows the river fairly closely, so the hiker doesn't miss much scenery, and the fisherman doesn't miss any likely spots. Of course caution should be used as there are many areas where it would be foolish to try to fish.

There are many places to wet a line along this stretch. Between the waterfalls every type of water is found: pools, runs, riffles, and pockets. My favorite spots to fish are in the pools below the waterfalls. However, be forewarned, you may miss some strikes at these sites due to the scenic distractions.

While planning my first backpack trip into this area I tried to find some fishing information on it. I drew a complete blank when checking books and magazines. Talking to other fishermen didn't help either. No one I talked to had ever fished it or knew anyone who had. The only information I could get was from the pastor of my church who had previously been assigned to Yosemite Valley. He's not a fisherman, but he'd heard of some huge trout being taken down in the Tuolumne below the meadows. It must be true, I decided, because who would lie to a priest (a fisherman perhaps)? Well, I didn't see any huge trout on that trip, but I really don't doubt that there are a few. My guess is that, like the meadow upstream, these rare fish are sometimes seen but seldom caught. It's a generally accepted premise that in a river that holds browns, there's a good chance that some will grow old, wise, and large.

White Cascade and Tuolumne Falls of the Tuolumne River. J.M. Olney, Jr. photo.

This part of the river sees lots of hikers but surprisingly few fishermen (with the exception of the Glen Aulin vicinity which does receive some fishing pressure). I found these fish to be very willing and not easily spooked—even in the pools. Most of my fishing here is done with dry flies, and as long as the flies aren't too big, I've averaged about five fish per hour. They are very colorful wild trout whose ancestors have been in the river for about 75 years. They aren't native fish, as the falls proved to be impassable barriers to ancient fish migration. But, due to the passing of time since the original planting of fingerlings, the fish have all the characteristics of natives.

I have found some sections of the river to contain only brookies, some to contain only browns, and some to hold a mixture of both. I have only caught one rainbow this far upstream, a surprise eight incher in a beautiful run below California Falls. I took the rainbow from the same spot that had provided brooks and browns minutes earlier. The brookies measure up to 10 inches, with the brownies averaging a couple of inches longer; some being quite fat. I haven't caught any fish, or seen any, over 13 inches in this stretch. Some of the summer employees at the Glen Aulin High Sierra Camp who fish river many days per year echo these findings. So, if it's big trout you're after, this isn't the place to find them. But, if you don't mind lots of willing fish in beautiful surroundings, it's worth the trip.

I haven't used nymphs too much here because dries work so well. There are abundant small mayfly nymphs and caddis larvae under the rocks in the river. Dry flies in sizes 12-16 work best, but again, the fish aren't too particular. Royal Wulff's and other white winged flies work well in the fast water where they are more easily seen than standard dry flies.

In some pools I played cat and mouse with the fish by letting the dry fly remain motionless after the cast. In very clear water I would watch the fish as it came up and refused the fly. I then would give it a couple of slight twitches. After a series of these encounters it would seem that we had reached a stalemate. But, more often than not, the fish would finally decide to hit the fly, and if I could resist striking too soon, the trout would be hooked. This game can only be played with fish that aren't too wary.

Anyone planning to fish the Tuolumne below Glen Aulin is advised to stay overnight if they wish to have any time to fish. If you do stay overnight, be prepared to hang your food out of the reach of the bears that live here. I saw three of these pesky critters on my last trip to the area.

Upstream from all these falls and cascades the river runs through one of the most beautiful places on earth, Tuolumne Meadows. At an elevation of 8,594 feet, it is the largest sub-alpine meadow in the Sierra, about five miles long and a mile wide. Snow-capped peaks surround the grassy meadow, and the river runs right through it. In this section the Tuolumne has the feel of the Firehole and Madison Rivers in Yellowstone. The fish in the meadows are almost all brown trout, with a few brookies scattered about. Again, they won't ordinarily be huge, but there are enough 10-12 inch trout to provide quality sport in this gorgeous setting.

Over the years I've heard all sorts of fish stories and rumors about monster browns in Tuolumne Meadows. Most of these fish were supposedly seen, not caught. In looking for hard evidence I've never seen either a mounted fish or even a picture of one of these alleged brutes. In fact, I had (after many fishing trips to the area) decided that they definitely didn't exist—or at least that they hadn't existed for the last 40 or 50 years. But one fall day in 1987 I experienced a sighting of my own. I was alone, of course—these things never happen with more than one person around—kind of like U.F.O. sightings, my wife was about a quarter mile upstream reading a book, and there was nobody else anywhere to be seen. I was creeping up to the bank preparing to try for a riser of about 10 inches when I happened to notice something out of the corner of my eye. A big dark shape swam from the bottom of the river toward me, and then disappeared under the bank I was standing on. It didn't seem to be in much of a hurry so I was able to get a good long look at it. The fish so dwarfed all the other fish I'd seen that I almost couldn't believe my eyes. But, it surely was a brown trout, and it was at least two feet long. I remember thinking that it probably would go six pounds or more. I stayed in the area for awhile, but it never showed itself again and refused all my offerings. You can now add me to the list of people who claim to have seen one of the Tuolumne Meadows mammoths. If anyone ever catches one of these they will truly have a fish to be proud of for the rest of their life. I feel privileged just to have seen one.

Now, getting back to catchable fish in the meadow, they will usually run from 5-12 inches. By far the best fishing method is fly fishing in this slow, clear water for these wary brown trout. The best fly to use is a Black Ant. I stumbled upon this fly when I caught my first ever trout here, and I've since learned that it is the top producer. Early in the season (June) a large flying ant is present in great numbers. It can be matched by using a size 12 black ant pattern with white wings. Later in the summer and fall small terrestrial ants abound, which frequently find their way into the water and are taken greedily by hungry trout. Trout love ants. The best results at this time are obtained by casting tiny (size 18-22) black ant patterns on long leaders tapered to 7X tippets. The water in the meadow requires delicacy, and only the best presentations will meet with consistent success.

The other winning method comes into play on breezy warm summer afternoons. This is grasshopper time. There are fair quantities of hoppers in the meadow, and some get blown into the river. If a big trout is to be caught here on a fly, this could very well be the fly that

The fast moving Dana Fork of the Tuolumne River.

does the trick. The fish aren't nearly as cautious when they see a big juicy hopper, so a stronger tippet can be used. Any hopper pattern in the size 10-12 range can be effective as long as it is tan and yellow.

Surprisingly, the meadow doesn't get fished heavily—despite the fact it is one of the most popular camping and hiking destinations in the entire Sierra. Part of the reason is probably due to the small average size of the trout, and to the difficulty in catching them. Still, I would expect to see more people trying their luck. The river near the campground is the only place I've ever seen more than one person fishing.

There are currently no special regulations in effect, so all methods, including bait fishing, are allowed. This is another place that I'd love to see limited to catch and release, although I'm not sure that this would greatly increase the average size of the trout. The meadows are inaccessible because of snow for six months of the year. The long winter limits the growing season of the trout, and the water is not tremendously rich in trout food. Also, the river currently gets fished, but certainly not overfished. So, with all this in mind, new catch restrictions probably wouldn't produce overwhelming results, but would most likely increase both the size and numbers of the trout by a small margin.

Tuolumne River Headwaters

The main Tuolumne River is formed in Tuolumne Meadows where the two main forks—the Lyell Fork and the Dana Fork—come together. The rivers' origins are in the upper crest of the Sierra on the extreme eastern side of Yosemite Park. The Lyell Fork originates near 13,114 foot Mt. Lyell, and is partly fed by the dwindling Lyell Glacier; one of the last remaining glaciers in the region. The Pacific Crest Trail (also called the John Muir Trail in this section) runs along the banks of the Lyell Fork for its entire length. The trail is never more than a

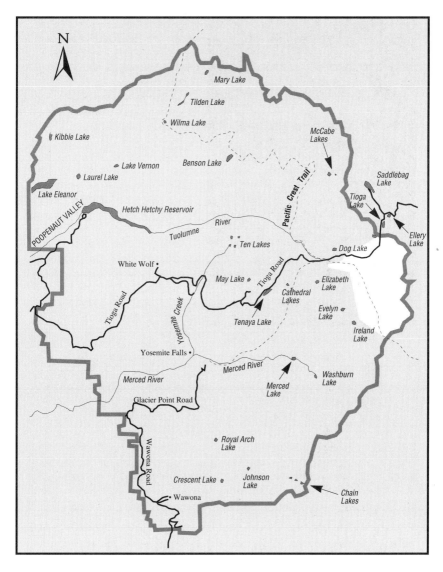

half mile away from the river—from the headwaters all the way down to Tuolumne Meadows, a distance of about 10 miles. The terrain is fairly level, so hiking from Tuolumne Meadows upstream is not difficult.

The Lyell Canyon is a scenic area and the river has a good population of wild trout. If it sounds like a good trout stream, that's because it is. What it isn't, is overfished. Though thousands of hikers walk the Pacific Crest Trail along its banks each year, surprisingly few take advantage of the fishing in the Lyell Fork. Of the few who do fish it, even fewer do a good job of it. There is some fishing pressure in the lower meadow section near the Tuolumne Meadows Lodge. A ten minute walk takes you to the river from the lodge.

I have a special affection for the lower meadow section of the Lyell Fork, for it was here that I landed my first trout on a fly. It was an eight inch brown that to me was more beautiful than any of the trout I'd caught while bait or spin fishing. It gave me special satisfaction to release this colorful wild trout (after a picture, of course) and watch it swim away. Looking back, I now realize that this meadow section was not a very easy area to catch my first fly rod trout. The water is smooth and the banks are open. The fish are very spooky although they regularly see many hikers along the Muir Trail. Here, as elsewhere, sometimes you can walk up to the bank without scaring the fish. But, raise your arm to cast, and the fish scatter like quail. Two lucky breaks allowed me to catch this fish. The first was that after a couple of unsuccessful hours of casting, a light rain began to fall. The rain ruffled the water's surface and disguised my sloppy beginner's casts. The second break was that my only remaining fly was a Black Gnat—a fly that I have since learned is a great one for this water. After that first fish, the light rain turned into a downpour and curtailed any further fishing for the day. As I made the wet hike back to my car, I was fully satisfied in the knowledge that I was now a fly fisherman. I probably would have achieved that satisfaction a little earlier if I'd only hiked a bit further upstream where the water wasn't so clear and smooth. Here you will find pocket water, riffles, and less selective fish.

I find that on a typical summer day almost any dry fly will get results. The most important aspect of the fishing is in a careful approach, and in determining the areas likely to hold trout. You should have success with dry flies in the 10-18 inch size range. I've caught equal amounts of fish with Adams, Mosquitos, Humpies, Elk Hair Caddis, and Royal Coachman patterns.

The trout population is rather scattered along the length of the stream. Some of the wide open, flat, featureless meadow sections hold few fish. Generally, more fish are found in the fast water sections and in the deep pools. Since the trail runs right along the river it is possible to cover miles of river looking for the best spots.

The fish will be mostly browns in the lower couple of miles near Tuolumne Meadows. The next few miles of river will yield a mixed catch of brookies and browns. The brook trout caught will outnumber the browns 2 to 1, but their actual populations are probably about equal. In the extreme upper portions of the river, only brookies will be found. Although rainbows have been planted many times over the years, they haven't done well in the Lyell Fork, and I've never caught one here. Brook trout were first planted in 1878 by early settlers and later by the Park Service. The early plants were very successful and brookies have flourished ever since.

An early account of the fishing in the Lyell Fork was reported by the acting superintendent of Yosemite. In his report to the Secretary of the Interior in 1905 he wrote: "No finer fishing can be found in the world than is had in this stream, nine miles in length, which runs through a continuous meadow and whose banks are clear of all growth. The depth of the stream varies from two to six feet, with many pools 20 feet in depth." At the time this was written brook trout were the main catch. Cutthroats were planted in 1896, but records indicate that they didn't fare too well. Brook trout did so well that adult brookies were netted here and transported to other park waters in 1905. Goldens were also planted three times from 1928-1938, but haven't successfully reproduced. Browns were planted extensively in Tuolumne Meadows from 1920-1948, and those fish have worked their way upstream into the Lyell Fork. Now, the biggest fish caught are browns. The brook trout go to about nine inches, and the browns get to about 12 inches.

Of course, there are a few trophy sized browns found on rare occasions. One of these, caught in the 1970s, is mounted and can be seen at the Tioga Pass Resort. This brute weighed eight and a 1/2 pounds and was taken somewhere in the Lyell Fork. Details are, understandably, somewhat sketchy. I'm sure there are a few more of that size in there somewhere. The trick to hooking up with one is to fish early in the morning or late at night. Fish of more than three pounds generally don't feed much during the daylight. You usually don't see these fish during the day either.

As you hike upstream into the Lyell Canyon through beautiful meadows, there are places where the water looks fishless. The water is clear and only an occasional brook trout is seen in the flat shallow areas. However, where cover exists in the form of rocks, logs, or undercut banks, larger trout may be lurking. Big trout are not found in feeding spots during the day, but after the sun sets they move to the shallows to feed. The small brook trout that most people try to catch during the day become targets for hungry browns at night. The best way to give yourself a chance at a big brown in the Lyell Fork is to hike in and stay overnight. This allows you to be on the water fishing during prime hours, instead of on the trail hiking. Big trout look for big meals, so fly fishermen should use streamers and spin fishermen should use large spinners and spoons when concentrating on these rare big browns.

Other successful flies for the average sized trout in the river include the White Miller—which is productive along the entire length. In the meadow sections Black Ants can be fantastic at times. In the warm summer months you'll find grasshoppers in the meadows. On breezy afternoons a grasshopper fished along a grassy undercut bank

Drifting dry flies on the gentle currents of the Dana Fork of Tuolumne River in Dana Meadows.

will sometimes produce nice trout. Trout much bigger than expected have a way of suddenly materializing under a big Hopper and lashing at it with savage greed.

Fish-worthy feeder streams to the Lyell Fork include Rafferty Creek and Ireland Creek. Rafferty is about two miles upstream from Tuolumne Meadows and holds colorful wild brook trout. The trail to Vogelsang follows the small creek all the way to its source. Trout in Rafferty seldom exceed 10 inches. Ireland Creek is a few miles further up the canyon. It also contains small brook trout, and also has a trail following it for much of its length. Both creeks can be fun to fish as the trout are wild and the fishing is solitary. Further up, Kuna Creek and Maclure Creek are generally fishless. Neither has ever been planted, and they only contain fish in their lower reaches—fish that have come up from the Lyell Fork. The best fishing in the area is found in the main Lyell Fork, a scenic uncrowded river that holds a few big trout for the fisherman to dream about as he hikes its beautiful banks.

The other main fork of the Tuolumne River is the Dana Fork. It originates near its namesake, 13,053-foot high Mt. Dana, and runs west to Tuolumne Meadows where it joins the Lyell Fork to form the main Tuolumne River. The Dana Fork carries less water than the Lyell Fork. The gradient is steeper so there is a lot of pocket and riffle water. There are also more trees on its banks than are found on the more open Lyell Fork. Highway 120 runs right by the stream along the entire length from Tuolumne Meadows to Tioga Pass. The road is never more than a few hundred yards away, and sometimes it is close enough that you could cast into the stream from the road. With such easy access it is again surprising to me that I don't see more people fishing this stream. It is a shallow stream with a good deal of fast water, so it is difficult water for spin fishermen. The fish are not tackle busters but there are plenty of them.

I think this is an ideal stream for a beginning fly fisherman. It's small enough that aggressive wading and expert casting aren't required to catch fish. The easy access means it isn't necessary to hike long distances from the road to find willing trout. A good example of this fact is the time I was staying in the tent cabins at the Tuolumne Meadows Lodge one June a few years ago. The lodge sits right on the bank of the Dana Fork. Before dark I thought I'd take a few casts to tune up for the next day's fishing. I walked right behind the dining room at the lodge and saw some trout finning in a pool. In less than an hour I'd had 20 rises to my dry fly. I caught and released 10 browns ranging from 6-11 inches. They continued to strike until it was too dark for me to see my fly and set the hook. Since I released all of them, anyone seeing me walking back with my fly rod and no fish must have said to themselves, "There goes that idiot who was fishing right by the lodge—doesn't he know you've got to hike miles into the wilderness to catch trout?" Well, that's not always the case, as I proved that evening.

This stream is not just for beginners either. It is such a delight to fish that anyone can enjoy it. It doesn't require a great deal of time or energy to fish, and the large numbers of trout anxiously hit dry flies all summer long. I like to stop here on my way back from the Eastern Sierra, particularly if the fishing was slow on famous trophy trout streams such as Hot Creek and the East Walker. It's good for the confidence to feel life at the end of the line after hours of unproductive casting. The gorgeous scenery makes up for the relatively small size of the fish. You also probably won't see another fisherman.

Three species of trout are caught in the Dana Fork: brown, brook, and rainbow. Rainbows have done better here than in the Lyell Fork because there is more of the fast water that they love. Rainbow and brook trout were planted often in this water—mostly in the 1930s and 1940s. Brown trout, which have worked upstream from plants in the main Tuolumne, dominate the lower sections. You rarely catch anything else from the junction with the Lyell Fork upstream to the lodge. Above the lodge the next few miles of stream hold a mix of the three species. In the pocket water rainbows will be the main catch. The slower water will hold brooks and browns. The rainbows and browns go to nine or 10 inches, with the brookies running a little smaller on average.

A little further upstream in Dana Meadows, browns and brooks

Looking down on Dana Meadows.

far outnumber the rainbows. This water is slower as it meanders through the meadow. The last time I fished here I caught mostly browns, a few brookies, and only one eight inch rainbow. It was an interestingly-colored fish though. It had very dark spots on its back and a deep yellow belly. In the extreme upper reaches of the stream only brook trout will be found. All the trout are colorful wild fish that hit almost any small dry fly. Small lures are also effective, but difficult to fish in the shallow water. Many different baits will work as these fish aren't too particular. At this high elevation they feed with vigor during the short summer growing period. They are accustomed to eating small insects because that is all that is available to them. A large fly or lure is more likely to scare them than to entice them into striking.

Bait fishing was outlawed on a three mile stretch of the Dana Fork in 1961. Yosemite experimented with "fish for fun" regulations here that called for artificial flies only, while only catch and release fishing was allowed. The results of angler surveys during this time showed that brook trout were the most common catch—outnumbering rainbow trout by a two to one ratio. It was also found that brook trout outnumbered browns ten to one. Since then I think browns have become a little more dominant. What hasn't changed is the size of the fish. Most of the fish reported in the surveys of 1961 were between six and eight inches, with a few between eight and 10 inches. Rarely was a fish reported to have been caught larger than 10 inches.

The tributaries to the Dana Fork are the Gaylor Lakes Branch and Parker Pass Creek. Each of these have trails following their courses. The Gaylor Lakes Branch is a small outlet stream draining the Gaylor and Granite Lakes basin. The stream is home to small brook trout of up to nine inches. The lakes were planted extensively with both rainbow and brook trout, but only the brookies now thrive there. Parker Pass Creek joins the Dana Fork near Dana Meadows. A good level trail joins the creek upstream about a mile from Dana Meadows—the Mono Pass Trail. Although the trail is level, the air is thin as the altitude is nearly 10,000 feet. It's a good idea to allow some time to get acclimated before setting off upstream. The pretty creek is small and has two types of trout in it—browns and brooks. Small dry flies are the most effective method for this creek, but stripping small nymphs also will draw strikes from most of the bigger plunge pools. The browns reach about 10 inches, while the brookies run a bit smaller. There used to be some golden trout in the branch below Bingaman Lake, but they are no longer present. The branch below Kuna Lake is loaded with small brook trout (5-8 inches) that will hit almost anything as long as they aren't alarmed.

There are six lakes in the Parker Pass Creek drainage area that hold trout. Kuna Lake is the closest, but in mileage only. A cross-country hike of three miles is required to reach it, and the hike is strikingly steep. This big lake has brook trout of up to about 12 inches. The brookies have reproduced from an early unofficial plant, but they aren't plentiful. Later plantings of rainbows (the last in 1966) have apparently not reproduced. The two Bingaman Lakes, Upper and Lower, are also reached by hiking cross-country. These are also brook trout lakes. Lower Bingaman has a healthy population of 8-11 inch brookies that, based on their willingness to strike, apparently don't see too many fishermen. Upper Bingaman was planted with goldens in 1958, 1963 and 1965, but they are probably all gone now. Only a small population of brook trout remains. Parker Pass Lake can be reached by trail and is about a six mile hike. It also has a small population of small brook trout.

The best lake in the area is Spillway Lake. It also can be reached by trail, and the hike in is about five miles. The trail to Spillway follows Parker Pass Creek all the way. A non-stop hike in would take about one and a 1/2 hours, except that the creek is so tempting with its riffles, pockets, pools, and meadow sections, that I can't resist taking a few casts on the way, and therefore, have never made it to the lake in less than two hours. The creek below the lake has a good population of browns that have come down from the lake.

The lake was planted with browns in 1945 and again in 1948. They originally did tremendously well in the lake as in 1949 a 30 inch, seven pounder was caught! Cutthroat, rainbow and brook trout have all been planted here at various times. Currently, the brook trout are the most common species caught, along with a small number of browns. I found the brooks to outnumber the browns about 10 to 1. Cutthroat and rainbow trout are no longer found in Spillway. The brook trout are common up to 12 inches, and an occasional 14-16 inch brookie is taken—near trophy size for a California brook trout. Far more browns are caught in the creek than in the lake.

Large nymphs on sinking lines work well for fly fishermen who wish to imitate the damselfly and dragonfly nymphs that are found on the lake bottom. Some good-sized trout can be taken if you're in the right place at the right time. This is a high elevation lake (10,450') that can only be fished a few months a year. I found small dry flies worked better than larger attractors, probably because Spillway does get visited regularly by fishermen. Size 18 Elk Hair Caddis, small black ants, and beetles can be very effective.

Following Spillway's inlet stream for about a mile leads up to Helen Lake. Helen, the largest lake in the area, offers solid fishing for medium sized brook trout. Not many fishermen hike up there, so the fish are easier to catch than at Spillway, although they are smaller (averaging about nine inches and seldom exceeding 11). Smaller flies work best, but these trout will hit most offerings. I found hundreds of rising fish on a September trip to this stark, windy lake.

Overall, these six are a very healthy group of brook trout lakes. Spillway has the biggest fish, with Lower Bingaman and Helen sharing the honors for most fish. A good pattern to follow when lake fish-

Spillway Lake from the west. Helen Lake sits in the bowl at the upper right.

ing with flies, which worked well at the lakes in this area, is to start with a large attractor in the 12-14 size range. I like the Coachman Trude because it's as easy to tie as it is to see on the water's surface. If you're getting refusals or missed strikes, you can switch to a smaller fly such as a size 16 or 18 Elk Hair Caddis, which is excellent as there are many caddis hatches on Sierra lakes. If the fishing is still slow, the next fly to try is a size 14-18 Black Ant or beetle. These are tough to see, but if the surface isn't too choppy, and the trout can see them, they seem to outproduce almost any other fly. Trout love ants and beetles. These flies cover most dry fly situations. A couple of Hare's Ears and Woolly Buggers round out the necessities, and are used if there is no interest in dry flies. These six patterns are usually all you need when dealing with unsophisticated wilderness trout. They probably cover 90 percent of all the fishing situations you'll encounter in the Yosemite backcountry, although I still carry hundreds of different patterns for that rare special spot where only a certain fly will do.

Tioga Pass Region

Shortly after leaving the beautiful Tuolumne Meadows area the road takes you to scenic Tioga Pass. Here, at nearly 10,000 feet (9,945'), there is a trail leading to the brook-trout-filled Gaylor and Granite Lakes. Middle and Upper Gaylor Lakes are reached by trail, while the two Granite Lakes are reached via an easy cross-country hike.

Lower Gaylor Lake can be reached by travelling cross-country from Middle Gaylor, or by taking the trail from the Tuolumne Meadows Lodge. Lower Gaylor teems with brook trout that reach the one foot mark. Gaylor Creek also is full of brookies of slightly smaller size. The lower portion of the creek also features rainbows mixed in with the brookies. Lower Gaylor, like the other Gaylor Lakes, was originally planted with rainbows in 1906. There were more rainbow plants in the following years and, additionally, plants of cutthroat trout were made before 1930. Presently, the three lakes feature brook trout exclusively. The brookies were first planted in 1937 and have found the Gaylor Lakes to be an ideal home.

Middle Gaylor, the biggest of the three lakes, is also the easiest to reach. A one mile hike from the Tioga Pass Entrance Station takes you to this high elevation lake (10,350'). As you might expect, this lake gets the heaviest use by fishermen, and accordingly, affords the poorest fishing of the lake group. There are still brook trout to be caught, they are just slightly smaller (to 10 inches), and less abundant. Effective flies for all the Gaylor Lakes are caddis and midge patterns. Small sizes match the naturals, but it is sometimes necessary to use bigger flies in order to keep track of them on the water. These high

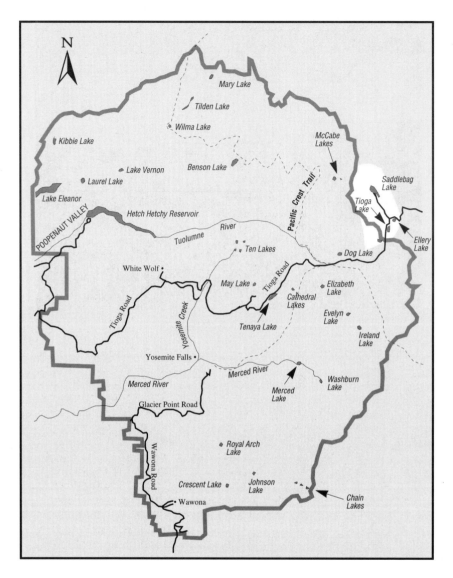

stark lakes do get a lot of wind and the water can become choppy, which makes it nearly impossible to see a small fly floating on the surface (it also makes it difficult for a fly to stay afloat).

Upper Gaylor abounds with brookies. The trout population is so dense that fly choice isn't too critical. As long as you don't scare the fish with your approach, you can catch good numbers of them in short order using a variety of methods. Most of the brookies will be between 6-10 inches, but a few reach the 12-14 inch range which

Middle Gaylor Lake.

adds a little excitement to the fishing. Fewer people fish Upper Gaylor than fish the lower lakes, no doubt discouraged by the steep climb. The hiking distances to these lakes are short, which attracts many day hikers and fishermen who may have just come from low elevations. They are expecting a leisurely stroll, but soon find their lungs aching and their heads pounding from the thin air. Many of these people make it no further than Middle Gaylor—the first lake they come to.

Two other nearby lakes that get less pressure than the Gaylor Lakes are Upper and Lower Granite Lakes. These are both solid brook trout lakes featuring good numbers of 6-12 inch fish. Rainbows were stocked in the Granite Lakes many times, but like the Gaylor Lakes, the brookies have prevailed. Fly fishermen should not be without small caddis dry flies when visiting this pair. Spin fishermen will find these brookies willing to hit almost any small lure—the smaller the better. A light line also should be used; nothing more than four pound test is needed.

The five lakes in this area are great places for beginning fishermen to hone their skills. They offer an excellent opportunity for the inexperienced angler to land some colorful wild trout. The scenery is outstanding, the lakes are easily reached, and the brook trout are plentiful. The fish in these high elevation lakes are opportunistic feeders, and when fished for at the right time will sock almost any fly or lure that comes their way. The early season is best, right after the ice melts, but these lakes will produce all through the short summer. Fall

Dana Lake, Dana Glacier and Mount Dana. This lake is reached most easily by mountain goats.

is always a good time to go after the spawning brookies as they are at their aggressive and colorful best.

Just outside the National Park boundary, Highway 120 skirts Tioga and Ellery Lakes. These are typical roadside lakes—complete with campgrounds and plenty of people. Since they are outside of Yosemite they are still regularly stocked with trout. Rainbows are dumped in both of them many times throughout the summer. Most of the fish taken will be the recent planters, but occasionally a holdover of good size is landed. A few wild browns live in Ellery Lake, and every once in a while someone catches a two or three pounder. Tioga Lake has a few wild brook trout that are mostly found near the Glacier Creek inlet. Glacier Creek itself is home to some wild brookies in its lower portion. A tough, very steep hike up this creek leads to the Dana Lakes. These four high elevation lakes (over 11,000 feet) sit at the base of Mt. Dana and the Dana Glacier. They are also sometimes called the Glacier Lakes. The lower two lakes contain small brook trout, while the upper two are home to the highly prized golden trout. The steep, high altitude hike and the lack of a maintained trail (which is non-existent in some places) discourage most people from trying for these pretty fish. Rarely does a fish from these lakes top 10 inches, but when fishing for goldens size isn't the key concern.

Near the Tioga Pass Resort (which rents cabins and stocks fishing supplies), there are some fun fly fishing spots. The creeks in the area hold small but willing fish. Tioga Creek and Mine Creek are home to brook and rainbow trout reaching about 10 inches. I've also taken a couple surprisingly big 11-13 inch browns from these tiny creeks. It's rumored that bigger ones are sometimes spotted—but rarely captured.

Saddlebag Creek also provides good fly fishing for browns in the 7-12 inch range. This creek runs along the paved side road that leads to Saddlebag Lake and Campground. At an elevation of 10,087 feet, this large lake has the distinction of being the highest lake in the state

In the Twenty Lakes Basin Saddlebag Lake is the biggest. Mount Dana, surpassing the 13,000-foot elevation mark, is the high peak in the center at the back.

of California that can be driven to on a paved, public road. Be prepared for cold changable weather if you camp there. At points along the road you can easily hike to the nearby brook trout lakes such as Shell, Mine, Fantail, Gardisky, and Maul. These lakes contain mostly small brookies, but local tales of the rare granddaddy squaretail coming out of them fuel the imagination.

Saddlebag Lake is regularly planted with rainbow trout, and most of the catch will be composed of these hatchery raised 8-12 inchers. To sweeten the pot, big brood stock rainbows also are put in the lake every year. In 1991 a seven 3/4 pound brooder was the biggest taken. The first day I was checking out the lake a six pounder was being weighed in. These may not be wild trout, but they still cause plenty of excitement around the area. There are a few small wild brook trout scattered about the lake, with the greatest numbers being near the outlet.

The Saddlebag Lake Resort rents boats and sells all the fishing supplies you need for the area. They also carry a good selection of fine flies. A good place to try those flies is the Twenty Lakes Basin, which is on the other side of the lake. You can take a water taxi across Saddlebag Lake (for a small fee) to save yourself some hiking. The Twenty Lakes Basin has lakes containing rainbow, brook, and golden trout, most of which are stocked by airplane once a year.

A few goldens have been taken from these lakes over the years that reach two pounds. Two pound goldens are altogether rare and are real trophies. One such golden is mounted and on display at the Saddlebag Resort. The resort can provide you with a good detailed map of the area.

Eastern Sierra Trout Wonderland

Highway 120 crosses Tioga Pass and steeply drops to join Highway 395 at the town of Lee Vining on the shores of Mono Lake. Highway 395 is the north-south link to the fine and varied fishing opportunities of the Eastern Sierra. Every type of fishing can be found here, from trickling creeks to raging rivers, from huge roadside reservoirs to pristine backcountry lakes. The waters run the gamut from the relatively unknown secret spots to the world famous trophy trout producers. Fishermen are limited only by their time, energy, and imagination.

The territory covered in this section is roughly parallel to Yosemite from its northern boundary to its southern boundary. There are certainly other fine fishing spots on either side of this section. To the north, the Sonora Pass area of Highway 108 features good fishing for rainbows, brookies, and browns in the West Walker River. The Emigrant Wilderness offers dozens of trout-filled lakes for the backpacking fisherman. Big brook trout are taken regularly at Kirman Lake and Poore Lake. Even grayling can be caught at Lobdell Lake, just north of Bridgeport. To the south of Yosemite in the Eastern Sierra, the Owens River and Pleasant Valley Reservoir produce fine catches of rainbows along with plenty of huge browns.

Besides these roadside waters, there are unlimited backcountry fishing locations between Highway 395 and Yosemite in the passes and upper crest of the Sierra. Due to practical limitations these areas will not be discussed in detail. It would take another book to thoroughly describe the fishing possibilities in the John Muir Wilderness, Ansel Adams Wilderness, Hoover Wilderness, and other areas of the Toiyabe and Inyo National Forests. Some of the trailheads and highlights of these areas are mentioned here, but are not covered comprehensively. Suffice it to say that there is also much quality fishing to be found in the places surrounding those covered in the following paragraphs.

Popular East Side Lakes

The lakes discussed here are all accessible by automobile. They are, therefore, quite well known and sometimes crowded. Additionally, each of them are planted with trout to supplement their wild trout populations. Most of these big, deep lakes will appeal to trollers and bait fishermen. They are difficult to fly fish effectively, but it can be done. As float tubes become increasingly popular, I'd speculate that many big fish will be taken in these lakes by fly fishermen in the coming years. One advantage that float tubes have over boats is their stealth. Most big trout in heavily fished lakes learn to avoid the shadows of boats and the sound of their engines. A quiet approach in a float tube can be a great way to sneak up on a trophy fish.

Starting in the north, the lake angler finds Bridgeport Lake. This big impoundment (3,000 acres when full) was formed by damming the East Walker River. The recent trouble has been that the reservoir hasn't been anywhere near full. Drawn down to provide water for farmers and ranchers during the recent drought, the fishing has been adversely effected in the lake as well as in the river below the dam. At times the lake looked like little more than a slow deep river. Even during the low water periods the lake still provides solid action for good-sized rainbows and browns. Most fishermen will use boats to troll or fish with bait. The cloudy water is home to some very fast growing trout, so it won't take long for Bridgeport Lake to rebound from the drought. The record is a 22 and a 1/2 pound brown, which shows the lake's potential for phenomenal growth. Many rainbows and browns in the 1-4 pound size range are caught each week during the trout season.

The Virginia Lakes are reached by taking Virginia Lakes Road off Highway 395 between Bridgeport and Lee Vining. This pretty setting has campgrounds and cabins are available. There is a resort on the lakes that sells fishing supplies and rents cabins. There are two lakes, Big Virginia and Little Virginia, both of which are regularly planted with rainbows. They also contain a few big wild browns. Big Virginia, the upper lake, also has a small population of native brookies. A four pound wild brookie was caught in 1977. Generally the brook trout are pan sized, and seldom grow larger than one pound. However, the browns do grow large. A 12 pounder has been reported from Little Virginia, while the big lake has yielded brownies to nine pounds. These wily giants aren't an everyday occurrence, but they do manage to turn up often enough to keep anglers interested.

Most fishermen use bait and spinners from boats and catch planted rainbows about a foot long. Fly fishermen should try streamers, sculpins, leeches, and matukas. The brook trout hit Royal Wulffs, Black Gnats, and mosquitos with equal abandon. The resort operator speaks of a mystery man who has great success fly fishing the lake from a float tube. Every fall he comes alone, in a black sedan, and consistently catches 4-8 pound browns. Those who know the secrets of these lakes can enjoy some fine brown trout fishing.

There is a pack outfitter located at the lakes, as they serve as a starting point for entering the Hoover Wilderness. Over the pass are some fine brook trout fisheries. Summit, Hoover, and Gilman Lakes are loaded with wild brookies in the 6-12 inch range. I had a good day catching those pretty fish after recovering from a bad bout of altitude sickness. The pass is over 11,000 feet, so although the mileage isn't great, it is still a difficult hike. My brother helped speed my recovery by landing trout after trout while I lay watching helplessly in camp.

The next lake south of Virginia Lakes off Highway 395 is Lundy Lake. Mill Creek was dammed in the early 1900s to form this reservoir. Lundy is heavily stocked with rainbows and also contains some very stout wild browns. Campgrounds and cabins are available near the lake. The Lundy Lake Resort general store has plenty of fishing tackle and groceries for the visitor. On opening day of 1991, a seven-and a 1/2 pound brown was caught in the lake. Fly fishermen should use sinking lines and weighted Woolly Worms or Woolly Buggers to get down to the big browns. The creek above the lake provides good fishing for 6-12 inch wild brookies. You also can hike into Lake Canyon and fish for the rainbow and brook trout of Blue, Crystal, and Oneida Lakes.

The June Lake Loop features drive-up fishing in four lakes. All four lakes, June, Gull, Silver, and Grant, are planted with rainbow, brook, and brown trout. Most of the catches are comprised of planted rainbows. Some of the rainbows planted are large brood stock fish like the 30 pounder that was planted recently in Grant Lake. In 1991, an eight pound brown was caught in June Lake.

Below Grant Lake there is a small population of wild brown trout in Rush Creek. New catch and release regulations may improve this fishery in the near future. There are some 1-2 pound browns caught in this stretch, and also an infrequent 3-7 pound holdover rainbow. It would be a great benefit to this area to have a high quality wild trout fishery nearby, so many people will be watching Rush Creek closely.

From Silver Lake you can enter the Ansel Adams Wilderness by trail. High above the June Lake Loop lie many trout lakes, including the golden-trout-filled Alger Lakes.

From the popular June Lake area head south on Highway 395 to reach the even more popular Mammoth Lakes region. Mammoth, the biggest town for miles around, has no shortage of motels, restaurants, gas stations, grocery stores, and fishing tackle shops. Some shops carry all sorts of fishing supplies while others specialize in fly fishing equipment.

The area lakes that make up the Mammoth Lakes group include: Mary, Twin, George, and Mamie. All are consistently planted with catchable sized rainbow trout. A few wild brown and brook trout also live in the lakes. Most people fish these lakes for the planters, and if you time it right, you can be there when big brood stock fish are planted. In late September the local merchants sponsor a trout derby in which over 2,000 rainbows from 3-5 pounds are released in the Mammoth Lakes. Some of these fish will holdover and be even bigger the following year.

Convict Lake.

From Mammoth there are several trails leading into the backcountry of the John Muir Wilderness. Fish Creek in Cascade Valley is just over Duck Pass. Hundreds of trout-filled lakes dot this wilderness area. Fine fly fishing for wild trout can be found in the Middle Fork of the San Joaquin River. Good sized browns and rainbows are found in the middle and lower sections, while colorful brookies and goldens live in the headwaters.

Convict Lake is just a few miles south of Mammoth and offers a chance for big browns. Convict is very similar to Lundy and the Virginia Lakes. That is, most of the fish caught are planted rainbows, but there are intermittent big browns landed every year. Enough anglers feel the tug of these cannibals on their psyche that more and more are showing up at Convict each year to try their luck. Big browns are well known as feeders upon planted trout, so a good way to tie into a hefty Convict Lake brown is to fish a large plug in the evening after the hatchery truck has dumped its load. The wild browns get big in a hurry when they feast on foot long hatchery fish. Large brood stock rainbows are also planted. These 3-6 pounders are too big to become a feast for the resident browns. In 1991, two eight pound wild browns were caught at Convict, and bigger ones are still in the lake. A photo in the State Fish and Game files attests to the size Convict Lake browns can reach. In a rather misguided effort to reduce cannibalism in the lake, the DFG netted as many adult browns as they could. The 1953 photo shows the awesome result of this project. A

The Sierra crest above Little Lakes Valley. Rob Olney photo.

dozen browns from 6-12 pounds are laid out for display, along with another dozen smaller fish. The Fish and Game people hoped that by getting rid of the predatory browns, smaller planted rainbows would have a better chance at surviving and growing. Luckily their effort wasn't entirely successful, and today there is still a chance at catching a wild, monster brown at Convict Lake.

Fly fishermen in float tubes give themselves an opportunity to hook a trophy brown when they use sinking lines and big flies. Various weighted streamer patterns work when cast in the early morning or late evening for browns of two or more pounds. Fish of that size generally feed on large prey (usually other fish) at night. Sunrise and sunset are often the only times an angler has a legitimate shot at hooking one of these submarines.

World Class Trophy Trout Waters

Cover stories for fishing magazines are written about these waters. People travel hundreds of miles to fish them. All five of these great fisheries are within an hour of Yosemite. They are so close together that it is possible to fish them all in a single weekend. Many of the biggest trout in the state come from these spots every year. They can get crowded, but it's possible to avoid the crowds if you stay away on weekends and on opening day. The following lakes and rivers can provide the angler with the fish of a lifetime at any moment. Fishing over tackle-busting fish can be exciting even when the catching is slow.

East Walker River

East Walker River has provided brown trout fishing equal to that of almost any river in the country. The river is in a rebounding stage at this time. When Bridgeport Lake was nearly emptied in August of 1988 by the Nevada Irrigation District, silt was flushed down into the East Walker. The result was devastating to the brown trout population. The eight miles from the dam to the Nevada border are the prime fishing miles of the river, and this section was virtually ruined as a fishery by the draining of the reservoir. The good news is that the river has been replanted and is on the road to recovery—in a few years it may be as good as ever. The silt will get diluted as it spreads out downstream. Also, the insect life looks to be in good shape. I fished the river about a year after the silting and found abundant mayfly and stonefly nymphs as well as caddis larvae under the rocks in the river. There is no shortage of food for them. The trout that were planted consisted of rainbows and browns in near equal numbers. Fish of up to 20 inches were planted. Bigger browns come down from the lake all the time. A year after the silting a seven pounder

Strong current on the East Walker River—waders beware!

was caught just below the dam. It won't be too long before the East Walker is again producing big fish on a regular basis.

How good was it? Well, six to eight pound browns were not at all unusual along the entire stretch of river. On any given weekend four and five pounders were almost a routine catch. Every day two and three pounders were taken. Most of the real big fish were browns, and the river record is a 13 pounder that was caught in 1967. The good rainbows were in the 14-20 inch range, and the average trout in the river was considered to be about one and a 1/2 pounds. Because of the abundant food the fish grew extremely quickly. Hopefully these fishing opportunities will return. There are already good numbers of two and three pound trout living and growing in this water.

As for the actual fishing conditions on the East Walker, let's just say it's not easy and it's not pretty. The river has a very fast current, so it is difficult to wade. But, wading is your only choice. It is too swift, shallow, and narrow to float. The banks are too brushy to fish from shore. I tried fishing it from shore years ago when I was a beginning fly fisherman. It didn't take me long to realize that this was a river for advanced anglers. I think more of my casts ended up in bushes than made it to the water. I didn't catch any fish and left without any flies either. Lesson number one: you have to get in the water to have any chance on the East Walker. When you do wade here you'll need felt soles or cleats on your wading shoes. Another must is a wading staff. I wouldn't think of fishing the river without these pieces of equipment. In addition to the swift current the rocks on the riverbed are slippery, as they are coated with moss, algae, and silt. During heavy flow periods wading can be dangerous and is only recommended for those with lots of experience. Even experienced waders can get into trouble, however. I once talked to an expert fly fisherman at a campfire on a Northern California river, when the subject of the East Walker came up his eyes brightened to match the coals of the fire. He told of taking a dunking and losing his fly box on the river. The next day he was swept away by the current and nearly drowned before he was able to scramble to safety. After a long pause he added, "Boy I love that river." The promise of big fish will do that to an angler. The secret is to keep your perspective and not lose respect for the powerful current. There are ample spots where the river can be waded safely and, if the aggressive wader takes only well calculated risks, he can increase his chances of landing a big fish while not decreasing his life expectancy.

The other problem presented by the East Walker is the brush along the river. It's thick and prickly on both banks at almost every point. Once you get to the water you'll want to stay in it as you fish upstream or down. This isn't always possible because of the strong currents—there are many places where wading is impossible. It is then necessary to battle your way through the tangle of brush and get away from the banks of the river. Then, moving upstream or downstream through the high desert chaparral (which is more passable a few yards away from the river), you again fight to regain the water. There are some trails that previous fishermen and cows have blazed through the thickets. These are a joy to find, although you may even be forced to crawl on them at places. Another tip that can save you aggravation and money is to wear wader protectors. Crawling through this brush is an easy way to poke a hole in your expensive waders. A pair of loose nylon sweat pants serves the purpose well.

One reason that the fishing has been so good on the East Walker is that it is so difficult to fish. Most people get discouraged after their first attempt, as I did. Another reason is certainly the rapid growth rate of the fish due to the abundance of food. A third reason, I believe, is the appearance of the river. It just doesn't look attractive. The water doesn't seem to jump out at you and say—"trout!" When I think of a trout stream I think of crystal clear pure mountain water. The East Walker is closer in color to a cup of coffee than to a glass of water. People driving by, even trout fishermen, would be unlikely to suspect that the river was full of trophy-sized trout. In fact, locals say that in the 1960s the fishing was tremendous but not too many people knew about it. Secrets, however, are hard to keep when they involve 10-12 pound trout. Even so, casual fishermen generally stay away from the river. The exception to this statement is at the pool just below the dam. The Big Hole, as it's called, is always crowded with all types of fishermen. This is the most accessible spot on the river, and nearly the only spot that can be fished effectively from the shore. This big, deep pool is most easily fished with spinning gear. The ease of fishing is one of the reasons so many people are drawn to the Big Hole. The other draw is the big fish that are caught there. More big fish come from there than from anywhere on the river, and there are two reasons for this. First, large trout come down from the lake and stay in this big pool. Second, spawning browns from downstream run up to the dam. It's a barrier for the spawners, and they are forced to stop there. The result is a large concentration of trout and a large concentration of fishermen below the dam.

The rest of the California portion of the river has good access. Highway 182 runs right along it, and there are ample pull-offs and dirt roads that will take you close to the water. Aside from battling through the brush, it is fairly easy to reach every part of the river. Much of the river is on private property, but the owners graciously allow fishermen on their land. It is hoped that people don't jeopardize this kindness by littering or vandalizing the area.

Even with its natural safeguards the East Walker does see quite a number of fishermen. Most fish the easy and obvious areas next to the road or near bridges. There are trout in these locations, but the crafty angler will seek out the more difficult lies. The big fish are found under the brush of the banks. These are the hardest places to put a fly, and will reward the best waders and casters. Hooking the fish is only half the battle, as there is a good chance the big browns will foul the leader on underwater brush and escape. The biggest one I've hooked did just that. I tried to keep him from heading for the sticks, but these brutes tend to call their own shots.

The angler should give himself a fighting chance by using a heavy leader of no less than 3X. People even use 0X tippets on these big fish. The advantage of the cloudy water comes into play, as the trout aren't leader shy. Sinking lines are also advised, for most of the fishing is done with big streamers and nymphs. The regulations call for only barbless, artificial lures. There is a two fish limit with a minimum size of 14 inches.

Popular flies include various streamers such as Hornbergs, Olive Matukas, and Marabous in white and black. To imitate the sculpin that big trout feed on, you can use Muddlers or the locally known Sierra Sculpin in sizes 2-8. Various other sculpin patterns also can be effective. The large stonefly nymphs are imitated with Bitch Creeks and Golden Stone nymphs in sizes 4-10. The Golden Stones hatch early in the season, so after the hatch smaller nymphs are more effective. Hare's Ears in sizes 12-16 are good for the smaller stoneflies and caddisflies that hatch on summer evenings. Tiny mayfly nymphs abound, but fishing tiny size 18 and 20 flies can be problematic. It's hard to get these little nymphs down deep in the fast current, and it's hard for the fish to spot them in the cloudy water. Still, when the big flies are drawing blanks, it is sometimes worth a try to put on a tiny nymph. A late summer breezy afternoon is a fine time to try a dry grasshopper pattern of size eight or 10. There are large amounts of hoppers on the riverbanks, and some do fall into the water. Explosive strikes may follow such an occurrence.

The best time to fish the river is probably in the fall when the browns are on the move preparing to spawn. At these times streamers catch the biggest fish. The season runs from the last Saturday in April to October 31st. The closing is two weeks earlier than the general stream closing in California of November 15th. By the end of October it is usually cool and often cold at this elevation (6,000 ft.), so pack warm clothes. There are hotels nearby in Bridgeport, but there are no campgrounds on the river. There are plenty of campgrounds on Twin Lakes Road outside of Bridgeport, but they are crowded for much of the summer. Sport shops in Bridgeport cater to fishermen and can provide any equipment you need.

Fishing in the East Walker has been great in the past, and there is no reason to believe that it won't return to that level in the near future. The river offers an opportunity for the angler to land a trophy trout in water that can be best termed as challenging. Every aspect of the fishing experience on the East Walker is challenging, and it is a type of fishing that tends to grow on you. If you hook a good trout here, whether you land it or not, you'll probably come back again.

Twin Lakes

While Scotland has its Loch Ness Monsters, California's monsters live in Twin Lakes. If you're after a state record brown trout, the Twin Lakes are where you should start. These two lakes, Lower Twin and Upper Twin, consistently produce huge brown trout. The current state record brown came from Upper Twin in 1987—it weighed 26 and a 1/2 pounds! The old state record was slightly smaller at 26 pounds. I'll give you two guesses where it was caught. No, not Upper Twin Lake, it was caught in Lower Twin Lake in 1983. Maybe that's why they call them Twin Lakes. Based on this track record it seems certain that the next record brown will also come from one of these lakes. There is probably a bigger trout in one of the lakes right now. Knowing that is one thing, landing the fish is another. Trout of this size are neither common nor easy to catch.

The Twin Lakes are located on paved Twin Lakes Road about a dozen miles outside the town of Bridgeport. There are several campgrounds on the lakes, but they do fill up. The lakes are scenic and are extremely popular with family vacationers as with serious fishermen. Bridgeport offers hotels and tackle shops for visiting fishermen. At the lakes you'll find a place to buy fishing supplies and rent boats. If you're hoping for a real big fish you'll want to have a boat, as most of the trophies are taken by trolling.

The current state record fish was reportedly caught by a die-hard troller who was out in a thunderstorm. This is strongly discouraged, but as I said earlier, big trout have a way of clouding people's judgement. Giving the angler the benefit of the doubt, maybe he hooked the fish before the thunderstorm started, and the long ensuing battle was waged during the rough weather. In such a case his behavior would be condoned by most fishermen. I know that if I had a trophy trout on my line it would take more than a thunderstorm to get me to abandon the fight.

Trollers use big minnow imitation lures and move them quickly through the water. The primary feed for the big browns in both lakes is small fish. These include the 6-12 inch kokanee salmon that are planted in the lake, as well as the rainbow trout in the same size range. The small planted rainbow and kokanee make up the bulk of the catch for most fishermen. Bait fishermen can have fun with these planters when fishing from the bank or from a boat. The usual baits take these fish; salmon eggs, power bait, and worms.

Fly fishermen can catch rainbows from previous plantings on dry flies. The best times for fly fishing are early and late in the day. The best success is enjoyed by fly fishermen who go out in float tubes and either watch for rising fish or fish the water with streamers. Risers will generally take any well presented small dry fly. These fish aren't used to seeing too many artificial flies, so they'll hit without reservation. There are a few good-sized wild brook trout in Upper Twin Lake, and float tubers sometimes get them up to two pounds. Float tubers using streamers such as Matukas and Woolly Buggers sometimes tie into browns reaching five pounds. The browns prowl the shoreline looking for minnows at dawn and dusk. The lakes are deep, both over 100 feet in depth, so the big fish have a sanctuary to retreat to during the middle of the day when the sun is threatening to them. They feel secure when the shadows fall upon the water, and it is at those times that they are most susceptible to something with a hook in it.

The best times of the year to fish Twin Lakes are early and late in the season. The first few weeks of the season (May) and the last few weeks (October) are the months when the most trophy trout are caught. The warmer months provide the best dry fly fishing because it is at these times that the insects are most active. There are no special gear or take restrictions in effect on either lake. Bait is allowed, but no live bait, and you can keep up to five fish per day.

The Twin Lakes offer good family fishing in beautiful surroundings. The wild card is the chance that your next cast may hook you up with a state record brown trout. Many a Twin Lakes fisherman has gone to sleep, under the stars, with that very thought livening his dreams.

Hot Creek

Hot Creek is an incredible little creek. It was the first nationally renowned fly fishing water in which I was able to catch a trout. As a beginner, I'd tried the East Walker and could hardly get my fly into the water due to the heavy current and brushy banks. I'd tried the Firehole in Yellowstone and could hear the educated fish laughing at my sloppy casts. I heard similar snickers at Hat Creek in Northern California. I tried to wade the McCloud River without a staff or felt soles, and couldn't get close enough to the fish to tell if they were laughing—I was slipping and sliding around like a first time ice skater. Why would a beginner try such famous, difficult water when he could be humiliated on his home water? The answer is simple: curiosity. You read about such places and just want to see them for yourself. Part of the fun of being on these well known waters is in watching other expert fishermen. You can learn from them while watching them catch fish. You hope to catch fish yourself, of course, but it's not mandatory. Much of the fun is just being there. You'd be satisfied to foul hook a six inch trout so you could say you caught a fish on a world class river, lake, or creek. This was my attitude when I went to Hot Creek for the first time as a rookie fly fisherman. My wife and I had been backpacking in the Eastern Sierra high country, and on our way home I convinced her to stop at Hot Creek. I'd heard

An uncrowded day on the public water of Hot Creek. It must be a weekday!

about the first rate trout fishing and she'd heard about the hot springs that sounded tempting to both of us after shouldering packs for three days. I was amazed to see so many fly fishermen in such a small area. My amazement increased tremendously when a trout took my fly. It was the middle of a hot August afternoon and I continued to catch fish until dark. I took five browns and two rainbows from 7-11 inches and thought I was a fly fishing legend. I soon found though, that I was surrounded by legends, because almost everyone was catching fish. It was astounding to see how many fish there were in this small creek. People fishing 50 feet from each other, constantly pounding the water hour after hour, day after day, and there were still enough fish to go around. I've been back often since then and have never been disappointed.

To get to Hot Creek you follow a good dirt road south of the town of Mammoth Lakes. The road first passes the state fish hatchery, which finds the even temperatures of the creek to be ideal for growing fish. The creek stays at about 55 degrees all year, allowing the fish to grow at a steady rate. The insects in the creek grow year-round, and the trout grow about an inch per month. It is a typical spring creek and has profuse weed and moss growth.

After driving past the hatchery you come to the private Hot Creek Ranch, a two and a 1/2 mile stretch of river that is owned by the ranch. You can rent one of their cabins and fish the creek with dry flies only. This is where the record trout of the creek was caught, a 14 pound brown taken on a dry fly. What a battle that must have been. The creek runs through a grassy meadow and is never very deep or wide. Hip boots are all you really need to wade it, although wading is not looked upon highly, and should be undertaken only when absolutely necessary. Most of the fishing can be done from the bank, as the creek is seldom wider than 40 feet.

The public water is only about a mile long and runs from the boundary of Hot Creek Ranch downstream to the hot spring bathing pools. Below this point the creek runs a few more miles before it joins the Owens River. This lower portion is too warm to support trout due to the hot springs. So, the fishable public section is only a mile long and is extremely popular with fly fishermen. Hardly an hour goes by during the open season (the last Saturday in April to October 31st) that there aren't a half dozen fishermen working the creek. Usually there are more, and Saturday evenings you have to stake out your spot. Sometimes there are 40 or 50 people trying to fish simultaneously, which works out to about one fisherman every 40 yards. The saving grace is that there are also over 11,000 fish per mile in the creek. The reason the creek stays so popular is that people still catch fish in these crowds.

Most of the fish are browns, although that wasn't always the case. The breakdown used to be about half rainbows, half browns. But, during the 1960s, plantings of Massachusetts brown trout were made, and they proved to be well suited for Hot Creek. These hardy fish now outnumber the rainbows eight to one. This trend is not likely to be reversed as the creek is getting warmer due to more water being diverted from cold water Mammoth Creek upstream. Browns tend to do better in warmer water than rainbows, so if the creek gets any warmer the rainbows may soon disappear. Hopefully the powers that be will realize the uniqueness and importance of the Hot Creek fishery and not allow its waters to warm to a point where all the trout are imperiled.

The average size for the trout is about 8-12 inches, with plenty of fish in the 12-16 inch range caught every day. The browns, on average, are a little bigger than the rainbows, and most of the big fish caught are browns. There are enough 18-20 inch fish in the creek to interest big fish hunters. Three pounders are caught from time to time, and five pounders aren't unheard of. The private ranch water tends to hold more of the bigger trout.

Fishing can be good at any time during the season, but after mid-July, weeds can cause a problem for nymph fishermen. Hot Creek is an ideal dry fly creek, but nymphs can be more effective when fished properly. Whether fishing dry or wet, flies should be small. Most of the insects these fish feed on are small mayflies and caddisflies. Fishing is restricted to barbless flies only, and is strictly catch and release—no fish may be kept. The last month of the season is also good—mainly because the summer crowds have thinned out and the fish aren't being constantly bombarded.

Long leaders with fine tippets are a prerequisite for consistent success as Hot Creek fish are very well educated. The big, old fish in the creek are Rhodes Scholars, and even the little guys are honor students. A 6X tippet is about as big as you should ever use. 7X, and even 8X tippets are used—sometimes on the ends of leaders over 20 feet long! A quiet, careful approach and a neat presentation of the fly are mandatory.

Small flies are the general rule, with few exceptions. There are midge, mayfly, and caddis hatches every month of the year. Most of these are best imitated with size 14-24 flies. One of the first mayflies of the season is the *Baetis*, which can be mimicked with Blue Dun or Blue Wing Olive dries in sizes 18 and 20. Later in the summer the tiny Trico mayfly hatches in the mornings. Trico spinner patterns in size 22 with brown bodies will match this little fly. A tiny gray midge hatches late in the season, and size 22 and 24 dries are needed to trick the trout that rise to them. Small Pheasant Tails and Brassies are good nymphs to use for the pre-hatch periods. These should be no bigger than size 18 for any of the mayflies or midges.

Caddisflies make up the bulk of the hatches on the creek. The different caddis types vary in size, from 12 to 20, their coloring is mostly in tan and gray tones. The Elk Hair Caddis is probably the most used fly in all sizes, but other caddis patterns are also widely used. More exact patterns use quill wings and include the Quill-wing Caddis, Kings River Caddis, and Henryville Special. Caddis pupae imitations that work well are the Sparkle Pupa and the more general Hare's Ear in sizes 12 to 16. Size 16 olive scud patterns also can be a good bet when nymph fishing. If I had to generalize and had a limited fly selection to take to Hot Creek, I'd want to make sure I had size 16 Elk Hair Caddis dries and size 18 Pheasant Tail Nymphs. With those two flies and a good presentation an angler should take a few trout if the fish are actively feeding.

Hot Creek is not a place for those who seek solitude while fishing. It does make a pleasant stop for a family, as the hot springs provide a soothing bath for non-fishing members. For the fly fisherman, the creek offers easy access, non-taxing fishing conditions, and abundant trout. Although crowded, Hot Creek is a unique fishery that should be experienced by every fly fisherman that has the opportunity. It often pays off in good-sized trout to those skilled enough to fool them. Yes, Hot Creek is an incredible little creek.

Crowley Lake

Opening day at Crowley reminds me of movies I've seen in history class of homestead land rushes—the ones where, after the gun goes off, families race their wagons across the plains to claim the best land. Others have likened the opening day to a zoo. Maybe the invasion of Normandy would also be a fitting description. In any event, opening day at Crowley is well attended. Thousands of fishermen converge on Crowley for the trout opener each year. At 5:00 in the morning, on the last Saturday in April, a flare is shot into the air to signal the beginning of trout season. It's kind of like the first pitch of the baseball season—a sure sign that spring has begun. Boaters and float tubers charge out into the lake for that first cast of the year. Surprisingly, the majority of them catch fish. Crowley is full of fast growing rainbow and brown trout.

The reservoir was formed in 1941 when the Los Angeles Department of Water and Power dammed the Owens River. The lake was named for Father J.J. Crowley, a Catholic priest who instilled hope in the locals that their surroundings weren't doomed by water diversion to L.A. He convinced them that the area could be promoted as a recreation area. If he were around to witness an opening day at his lake, he would see that the promotion has been a success.

Fishing regulations at Crowley change halfway through the season. From opening day until July 31st there are no special restrictions. Any method may be used, and up to five trout may be kept. From August 1st until the season closes on October 31st, only barbless hooks may be used. Additionally, during the trophy season, a two fish limit is in effect and the minimum size limit is 18 inches. Motor boats are allowed, and can be launched from the boat ramp on the southwest side of the lake. There are a dozen campgrounds within a short drive of the lake. These range from modern trailer parks with showers and laundries to primitive tent sites with no running water. The 5,000+ foot acre lake sits at a 6,781 elevation, so it does get cold early and late in the season.

The browns and rainbows share the lake with Sacramento perch. The perch get big enough that they are fished for, but their importance to trout fishermen is when they are small. The abundance of perch fry is the main reason that Crowley Lake trout grow so fast and so big. The trout gorge on the perch fry, which allow them to double their size in one year. Crowley is planted regularly, and a one and a 1/2 pound trout will be three pounds the next year. The rainbows reach five pounds in weight and 30 inches in length. The browns get bigger—some reaching 10 or even 15 pounds. Most of the good fish caught are between 18-24 inches, with plenty of one and two pounders available. The fish feed on insects, but the perch make up the bulk of their diet. About the time the regulations change the young perch are big enough to make a mouthful for the trout. This is the time things begin to get interesting for the fly fisherman at Crowley. The primary method of fishing at this time is to work the weed beds along the shore. The big, hungry trout begin prowling the shore for perch fry, and the savvy fisherman is ready with imitations of their prey. Most people use float tubes, but shore fishing also can be effective.

Various patterns can be used to imitate the perch, in colors of olive and brown, and in sizes from 4-10. In August size 10 is usually about the size of the naturals, in September size eight works, and by October the perch have grown to a size best imitated with number four or six hooks. Many local patterns have evolved to match the perch fry. Popular well known ties include Matukas, Zonkers, Woolly Buggers, and Leeches. Whatever fly is used, the key is to approach the fish quietly.

A big trout in shallow water is usually a cautious trout that can be easily spooked. If you find a feeding trout that isn't scared by your cast, it may hit your fly hard. A trout chasing a fish will usually sock it viciously, and a strong leader is needed to absorb the force of the strike. A 3X tippet is as light as you should dare to use. A sink tip line with a medium length leader is a popular choice for fly fishermen. Ideally, you cast toward a trout you've spotted, and strip in the fly in the manner of a swimming minnow. If a big fish strikes you don't need to set the hook hard—just raise the rod tip and you should have him.

There are some places on the lake that are better than others, but anywhere you find weeds you may find perch fry, and anywhere you find perch fry you'll probably find trout. The best producing area is the narrow northern part of the lake. Trout preparing to spawn and returning from spawning move through this section in the spring and fall. Unpaved turn-offs from Benton Crossing Road will take you to the lake. The west shore can be reached by turning to the right off Benton Crossing Road soon after leaving Highway 395. The east shore is accessed by following Benton Crossing Road as it crosses the Owens River. The road forks as it crosses the river and you turn right there to follow the lake's east shore.

Fly fishermen who enjoy lake fishing should enjoy Crowley. The lake is big enough to accommodate hordes of anglers, but usually you can fish in relative solitude. Boating fishermen enjoy miles of productive water to troll, while float tubers seek out hot areas that they can work thoroughly in private. Bank fishermen also can find success in the shallow, weedy shoreline. Crowley has plenty of trophy sized trout waiting for all types of fishermen using all types of methods. There are innumerable fishermen who list Crowley as the place where they caught their biggest trout.

Owens River

The Owens River may very well be the most heavily-fished river in California. It runs along extensively-traveled Highway 395 for nearly one hundred miles from its headwaters in the Mono Basin to the town of Lone Pine. In the area near Independence the water is diverted to the Los Angeles Aqueduct where it is carried to thirsty Los

Angeles. Anglers try for bass and trout along its entire length, including the three reservoirs it has created.

The lower river, from Crowley Lake to below Pleasant Valley Reservoir offers miles of fine fishing for rainbows and browns. The river is open all year and yields catches of wild trout to 20 inches. The upper river is also an excellent fishery with numerous tackle busting trout to be had. It is the upper river that I will focus on. The Owens River is a huge spring creek. Deadman Creek is joined by three large springs near Crestview. This area, called Big Springs, is considered to be the headwaters of the Owens. Much of the Upper Owens is on private property. Big Springs begins the first stretch of public water, and has a good campground located right on the river. The public can fish from there downstream for about a mile, where the river runs through the private Alper's Ranch. Next comes the private Arcularius Ranch, then the water is again open to the public for the final five miles before it enters Crowley Lake. The whole upper river is at its best early and late in the fishing season, as most of the big fish come up from Crowley on spawning runs. The trick is to find out where these fish are most concentrated at a given time. The spawning fish commonly range from four to eight pounds, although not too many of that size are landed. Many two and three pounders are taken during the spring and fall runs. In the middle of the summer many smaller resident trout are caught, most in the 6-12 inch range. There are some large resident trout best spots, but the fish are small in number and extremely shy and cautious. Very few such trout are hooked, and fewer still are landed. There are more big resident fish found on the private water where all fish must be released (many in the 15-20 inch range) but even there the spawning runs greatly increase the odds ot tying into a torphy.

The regulations change during the fishing season to protect the spawning runs. From opening day (the last Saturday in April) until May 31st there is a two fish limit, an 18 inch minimum size requirement, and a barbless artificial hooks only restriction. From May 31st until October 1st there are no restrictions; general rules apply. Then, from October 1st to the October 31st closing, the early season restrictions again apply.

It is during the times of the more stringent regulations that the fishing is best. Early in the season the spawning rainbows can usually be found in the headwaters area near Big Springs. This part of the river is brushy and fast, and is most easily and most effectively fished with nymphs. Caddisflies dominate the river, so caddis pupa patterns are appropriate, as are general patterns such as the Hare's Ear. These should be weighted and fished in sizes 10-16. In late May the rainbows will be leaving this area and returning to the lake. Fishermen with reservations on the private ranch hope to time the downstream run. The water on the ranches is slower, featuring more pools and

Wide open Owens River above Crowley Lake.

runs than riffles and pockets. Fishing methods in this section, at this time of year, usually consist of using sinking lines and big flies. Streamers are the first choice of the majority of anglers, the most commonly seen include: Woolly Buggers, Leeches, Matukas, and Hornbergs. The same methods apply on the last stretch of public water above Crowley Lake. This five mile stretch is flat, open pasture land. The river is slow and the fish seek protection in the undercut banks. Those are the areas to carefully probe with your streamer flies in hopes of luring a big spawning rainbow to strike. June can be a good time to fish immediately above the lake. July and August usually don't produce many big fish from any part of the upper river. There are plenty of small trout in the river all year, but the better fish stay in the lake during the summer. Most of the small resident fish are rainbows, which outnumber the browns about four to 1. The Fish and Game electroshocking survey done on the Arcularius Ranch in the 1980s showed over 11,000 trout per mile. Incidentally, the private ranches carry their own fishing regulations that are more strict than the state's. For example, the Arcularius Ranch allows only fly fishing and requires that all fish must be released. They also discourage wading except to cross the river.

Late September usually finds big fish again moving upstream to spawn. These will be mostly browns, although there are fall-spawning rainbows in the system. Early October is a good time to hit the public water just above the lake. Fishing methods are the same as those in the spring—sinking lines and big streamers in sizes 2-6. As October rolls along the fish move into the private water. You must book far in advance to get a cabin during this prime trophy trout time period. If you aren't able to get a reservation on the private water you just have to hope that the run of trout will reach the Big Springs public water before the season closes. Some years it happens; some it doesn't. But, the closer to the end of October you fish the upper public water, the better your chance at getting into some big browns. Large nymphs and streamers are considered to be the most effective flies to elicit angry strikes from the spawning trout.

Big Springs is reached by taking the Owens River Road for two miles from Highway 395. The turnoff from the highway is located about halfway between June Lake and Mammoth. This part of the river is very pretty and is lined with trees. The water reminds me of Hot Creek without the weeds and with more water. The public water immediately above Crowley Lake is found by following Benton Crossing Road from Highway 395 south of Mammoth. There is a public campground at Benton Crossing right on the river.

The healthy fast-growing trout of Crowley Lake are most vulnerable to fishermen when they enter the Upper Owens to spawn. In the spring and fall this winding, grassy river harbors trout of heart thumping size. You'll see the huge browns and rainbows in the clear, slow water, and their images, now permanently etched in your mind, will draw you back to the river.

Little Known East Side Creeks

Most of the creeks that drain the high country and run into the Owens River contain trout. Most are planted regularly with rainbows, and from time to time some of the planters are quite large. The big brood stock trout are usually put in lakes, but they are also sometimes put into creeks as well. Some rainbows found in the creeks are holdovers from previous plantings. Not many stocked trout survive (they're either caught quickly or die because of a lack of survival skills), but the ones that make it a few months begin to take on the characteristics of wild trout. They get more colorful, stronger, and more wary. The hatchery fish aren't afraid of people, but it doesn't take them long to learn that fear.

Most of the creeks also hold wild trout. From Robinson Creek in the north near Bridgeport, to McGee Creek south of Mammoth, there are creeks that provide great sport for fly fishermen as well as bait fishermen. I've fished most all of them in the last couple of years and have found, I'm happy to report, that the wild trout seem to be surviving the drought. Although in some cases there are fewer fish or smaller fish because of the low water, generally they are in pretty

Rush Creek lives up to its name.

good shape. A couple of normal precipitation years should be enough to restore these hardy fish. As long as a fair number survive, the streams get replenished (another reason to release all wild trout caught). I have found brooks, browns, and rainbows in these creeks. Some hold one species, some a combination of two, and some contain all three species. Some even have goldens in their upper reaches making them 'Grand Slam Creeks'.

One creek that is home to brooks, browns and rainbows (the 'Triple Crown') is Green Creek. Draining Green Lake into the East Walker River near the town of Bridgeport, this creek offers a variety of water types for a variety of trout. A dirt road runs along the creek in its upper stretches, so access is good even if the road is a bit rough. It is passable for two wheel drive vehicles if it isn't too muddy. I once had to wait 15 minutes for a shepherd to get his sheep across this road, so be prepared for possible delays. Along Green Creek Road the creek can be seen changing character. At some places it's rocky and steep; at others it's slow and brushy. Some spots are steep and brushy which makes for difficult fishing. More often than not these tough places hold wild trout in good numbers because they seldom get fished. Even less seldom do they get fished well. Green Creek also has some areas where it runs through beautiful meadows. These areas are tough to fish because they are so open—making the trout hard to approach.

The brookies are generally small (as brookies are prone to be), while the rainbows and browns are bigger. There are enough good-sized rainbows and browns in the 10-14 inch range to make things interesting. Things get even more interesting on occasion. Every once in a while a big brown is landed, such as the four pound brown that was pulled out in 1991. A very strong line would be needed to land a fish that size in such a small creek. It could well be the highlight of a fisherman's career. There are a few of these big browns waiting for the lucky and skillful angler. A variety of dry flies may be successful on Green Creek as long as they are small. Sizes 14-18 caddis, mayfly, and general attractor patterns all work when presented properly. There is a campground at the end of the road that often fills up. Above the campground you can hike along the creek where mostly brook trout are found. The trail leads to a few lakes that can be reached via short hikes. Green, East, and West lakes all contain trout.

Perhaps the most popular creek in the Bridgeport area is Robinson Creek. It flows along a paved road that leads to the famous Twin Lakes. There are several campgrounds along the creek that are needed to accommodate the continual flood of visitors. Many campers fish Robinson Creek for its planted rainbow trout. Happy campers find salmon eggs, worms, and power bait will entice the hatchery fish. The toughest and best spots do harbor a few wild browns. These are rarely caught. Some good browns come down from Twin Lakes and are sometimes taken. Above the lakes the creek contains wild brook trout. The further upstream you hike the more brookies you'll find, and most are in the 6-10 inch range. Small caddisflies are probably the most effective choice, and most of the fly fishing is done with dry flies on this small creek.

Heading south the next drainage is Virginia Creek. Like all of these Eastern Sierra Creeks, Virginia has an extremely steep gradient. But, there are some flat miles in the lower part where the creek runs right along the highway. It is down there that you can find some beaver ponds that have some foot long brook trout. There are quite a few beavers working this drainage, including one huge animal of about 70 pounds. The hard to reach parts of the creek hold the wild brookies. There are also a few wild rainbows (including big holdovers) and browns periodically taken, but most of the fish caught are smaller planted rainbows. The hard to reach places are both brushy and far from the road. Most of the creek is brushy and difficult to fish so be prepared to lose your share of terminal tackle. The wild fish are easily spooked, so a light line is called for. This creates a problem as the light line breaks easily when snagged on the magnetic streamside trees and bushes. If you're looking for easy fishing you should stay away from these Eastern Sierra Creeks.

Mill Creek is the small creek that was dammed to form Lundy Lake. Above the lake Mill Creek is home to small brook trout. A 10 incher is a rarity and a 12 incher is a prize. The bigger brookies can be found in the beaver ponds above the lake. Below the lake, Mill

A three pound rainbow, like the one above, can put on a great show when hooked in a tiny creek.

Creek is a typical Eastern Sierra run-off stream, that is to say—it's brushy and fast moving. There are some nice wild browns in the creek along with plenty of planted rainbows. I took plump, colorful, hard-fighting, wild browns up to 12 inches from the best-looking spots in the hardest areas to reach. Campgrounds all along the creek provide many trails and easy access to the water. Ignore the easy spots when searching out the brownies. A 12 inch brown in this small brushy creek is a handful. A five pound brown was caught in the creek a few years ago (some fish get sucked through the dam out of the lake). It's something that happens rarely, but could happen again.

The next major creek you come across is Lee Vining Creek. It originates from Tioga Pass and empties into Mono Lake near the town of Lee Vining. The creek runs through a picturesque meadow that you look down on from Tioga Road (Highway 120). There are many popular campgrounds along the creek. Unfortunately, all the camping activity has hurt the wild trout population through years of heavy fishing. The creek is now regularly planted, and the wild fish are in the minority. According to local old-timers, Lee Vining used to be a fine brown trout stream that even produced one pounders on a consistent basis as recently as the 1970s. Now, the wild browns are few and far between. Your best bet is to get away from the campgrounds and carefully probe the secluded holes. It's still possible to get your share of 10-12 inch browns if you work for them. A few bigger browns are sometimes seen. Although the wild trout fishing isn't what it used to be, this is a pretty spot for those interested in fishing salmon eggs for hatchery rainbows.

Walker and Parker Creeks are both very small and brushy. This makes for tough fishing conditions and small trout. Both hold some wild trout, mostly browns in the 6-9 inch range. There is very little water in these creeks, and finding little pockets to cast into can take more time than you spend actually fishing. There are a couple of pools on Walker Creek where the fish congregate, but the trout will still be small. These spots are also well known to locals who fish them regularly and keep the fish from getting too bold. I was surprised when I happened across one of these holes—seemingly in the middle of nowhere—to find selective trout that were difficult to fool. Scattered salmon egg and worm cans soon clued me in to the reason. Neither of these creeks will probably get any repeat business from me, but it was fun checking them out once.

South of June Lake you can find quiet uncrowded camping on Deadman Creek. A few miles on a dirt road leads you to the campground on this tiny creek. It is planted regularly at the campground, and does hold a small population of small brook trout that seldom exceed seven inches.

Moving further south brings you to the Mammoth Lakes area. Most popular for skiing, it's also getting better known as a fishing destination in the summer. The majority of fishermen who visit try the Mammoth Lakes themselves. Fly fishermen usually hit nearby Hot Creek. A fine and relatively unknown river (unknown to visitors, not to locals) that is close to town is the San Joaquin. The San Joaquin is an especially good river for the wading fly fisherman who likes fast water. It holds plenty of 6-12 inch browns that are usually quite willing to hit dry flies all summer long. Good caddis hatches abound, so bring some Elk Hair Caddis in sizes 12-16. There are also rainbows planted in the campground area of Devils Postpile National Monument. Upstream from there, the hiking angler can have a good time catching dozens of colorful rainbow/golden hybrids.

There are a few lesser known creeks near Mammoth that can be fun. Sherwin Creek and Mammoth Creek are regularly planted and draw the bulk of the fishermen to them—especially Mammoth Creek as it passes right through town. Mammoth also has some wild browns and a few wild rainbows that are found in the hard to reach spots. It can be tough to cast due to the brushy overgrowth, but with talent and persistence, you can find a rare 12-14 inch brown in this small creek. An even smaller creek is Laurel Creek. Just out of town I took an 11 inch brown in less water than you'd take a bath in, and a 10 inch rainbow in a spot barely wider than a foot across. I'm still not sure exactly why I even tried to fish there, except that I have a thing for small creeks. Hilton Creek also holds wild browns in its upstream

Devil's Postpile on Middle Fork San Joaquin River.

reaches that average 8-9 inches.

Convict Creek, south of Mammoth, is another somewhat lightly fished creek that holds wild trout. It too is stocked near bridges and campgrounds, but getting away from those areas can provide solitude and pretty trout. The creek is swift and brushy below Convict Lake until it crosses the highway and flows into Crowley Lake. In this brushy section I caught some pretty little browns with butter yellow bellies, but I had to work for them. There is also known to be a smattering of wild brookies and rainbows in the creek—although I've caught only browns. In the fall some huge browns from the lake move into this small creek and provide thrills for anyone who sees them. They are rarely caught, even less so in recent years since there are less browns in the lake than there used to be. A couple of these monsters are on display at the Convict Lake Resort. They were caught in the creek during the 1960s—one went 12 pounds. I'd have paid to watch that battle in this little creek.

Down the road from Convict Creek you next reach McGee Creek. McGee Creek Road follows the creek upstream to a campground, a pack station, and a trailhead. The trail climbs to the spine of the Sierra and joins the Pacific Crest Trail. McGee Creek has a little better head of water in it than Convict Creek. It mostly houses browns in the lower stretches, brookies up higher, with a sprinkling of rainbows throughout the entire length. There is no big lake to feed huge fish into the creek as at Convict. The McGee Lakes are far upstream and are fairly small. The creek's rainbows and browns reach about 12 inches, while the brookies top out a couple of inches smaller. Again, casting is difficult so this is not a creek for beginners. The best fish are protected by tangles of brush and canopies of trees. Small dry flies that float well are of utmost importance on this, and most of the creeks in the area. Humpies, Irresistibles, and Wulffs fit the bill nicely and will all draw strikes.

Rock Creek is the furthest south I'll travel. It drains the gorgeous high country of Little Lakes Valley. In the upstream area you find small brook trout (5-8"). Further downstream, along the road, are planted rainbows and wild browns. This creek is very heavily fished, but qualifies as a lesser known creek because 99 percent of those who fish it are pursuing the planted trout near the plentiful campgrounds. Fishing between the campgrounds, away from the road, you can find fair numbers of decent sized wild browns. Most are from 6-9 inches, but with a little hard work you can extract some in the 10-12 inch range.

There are some open areas near the campgrounds on these east side creeks that feature smooth water and allow beginners to try for hatchery fish. Such spots are heavily fished day after day during the trout season. However, the tougher spots go unfished for weeks at a time. The little known wild trout fishing in these creeks can be fun and rewarding for the angler who is willing to put forth the extra effort that is required to be successful.

On one of the creeks discussed in this section I hooked a brown trout of about 18 inches. I can't disclose which creek it was for the following reasons: a) maybe it was a fluke, and sending someone there would be like sending them out for the pot of gold at the end of the rainbow b) I didn't land it—maybe it was smaller than 18" (although I did get a good look at it) c) it's such a small creek that it couldn't handle the fishing pressure if everybody knew how good it was d) I don't want to deprive anyone of the fun of searching for themselves. Although I didn't land the trout, the search for such a big fish in such small water is an exciting bonus to go along with the solitude and beauty found in these relatively unknown jewels.

I hooked, and did land, a rainbow of similar size (the fish weighed about three pounds) in one of these creeks on a memorable September day in 1993. This trout was caught in a hole about the size and depth of a bed mattress. It seemed to know there was no way out as the hole was choked off from below by a fallen tree, and above by rocks. It confidently took my size 14 Adams and surprised me (shocked might be more accurate) with its size. I was expecting maybe a 10 inch brown, and hoping for one of twelve inches. When the fish struck I saw its outline and thought I had the jewel of the creek, a 14 inch brown. When it leaped half out of the water I saw I was pleasantly mistaken. The red stripe on this male rainbow was distinctive, wide and deeply colored. The back and belly of the trout did look like a wild brown though. The back was more brown than green, and the belly was a definite yellow, matching the color of the creek bottom. It was by far the biggest trout I've taken in this small creek. Although I probably shouldn't disclose the exact spot (for the same reasons as before), I will give a few clues. It is a creek that drains a lake and is found between Lee Vining and Bridgeport. The creek has the same name as the lake(s) it drains. That narrows it down a little, but there could still be some doubt. Here's a final clue in the form of a riddle: "Yes, young girl, there is a Santa Claus."

No one writes cover stories on creeks like these, nor do people travel hundreds of miles just to fish them. However, sometimes less heralded spots can salvage a trip when more glamorous waters fail to produce. These creeks have come through and saved the day for me on more than one occasion.

Top Ten Fishing Tips

1. When choosing a fly, think light for rivers and creeks, dark for lakes. The light colored wings and bodies are easy to see for both fish and fisherman. In still water visibility isn't as important, and dark colored flies match the ants and beetles that are often encountered and always savored by trout.

2. If you're not a fly fisherman, consider using a casting bubble and a fly with your spinning rod. This is particularly effective on hard fished waters where trout see so many spinners and spoons that they'll ignore them, and in crystal clear waters where large lures will scare them.

3. Consider using two flies at once: one big, one small. In addition to giving the fish a choice, you get the trout's attention with the big fly, and if it won't strike at it, it may take the small fly that is closer to the size of its natural prey.

4. Look for bubbles on the surface of still water when you can't see rising trout. On the choppy surface of a wind blown lake you may not be able to see fish rise, nor can you see the telltale rise rings. However, a rising fish often leaves bubbles where it has taken an insect off the surface, and these can give away its position.

5. Where possible, fish a lake with the sun in your face keeping your shadow off the water, and fish moving water by making your way upstream. Trout lie facing the current, and leave a blind spot behind them where they are more easily approached.

Popular flies for fishing Yosemite: (left to right) Woolly Worm, Pheasant Tail Nymph, Gold Ribbed Hare's Ear Nymph, Grasshopper, Mosquito, Adams, Elk Hair Caddis, Royal Wulff. All flies tied by author.

6. Adopt a hunter's attitude when looking for big trout (especially big browns)—you need to sneak up on these fish.

7. Buy good quality flies. Cheap flies (dry flies in particular) are next to worthless.

8. Carry more flies and fly patterns than you think you'll need. They don't take up much space, and are nearly weightless. Nothing is worse than hiking long and hard to reach a fishing spot and then finding that you don't have the right fly.

9. Search out the tough spots—it often pays big dividends. Cross over and fish the opposite side of the river. Go to the opposite side of the lake from the trail and campgrounds. Follow creeks away from trail crossings—sometimes you only need to go a few hundred feet to find much improved fishing. Go cross-country to lakes that have no trail access. Wade aggressively in rivers to reach spots that may go unfished for years.

10. Carry waders and wading shoes. These items can give you a huge advantage over fishermen who don't get into the water. Water at high elevations can be ice cold so you won't be able to wade wet for more than a few minutes at a time. Waders allow

Unidentified sailor with a large brook trout at a backcountry lake in Yosemite. Circa 1940s.

you to stay in the water longer, stay dry, and reach the fish that shore anglers can't—fish that often cruise (uncannily) just out of casting range for bank fishermen. Good lightweight waders are available from a variety of manufacturers. Good lightweight wading shoes are harder to find—most are too heavy to reasonably carry on a long hike. A solution to this problem is to make your own out of a pair of old tennis shoes. Just glue Indoor/outdoor felt carpet onto the bottom of the shoes using contact cement. The light shoes will give you good footing when fishing over rocky-bottomed waters. They can also be used to ford rivers and creeks, keeping your hiking boots dry. An additional use is as a camp shoe. It's nice to be able to take off your hiking boots after a long day on the trail and put on lightweight tennis shoes.

Top Ten Tips For the Trail

1. Bring a couple of small water bottles rather than one big one. If you get a leak in one you'll have another to fall back on.

2. You can never have enough matches in different places on your person and in your pack. My wife laughs at how many different pockets and pouches I put matches in, but when I'm out by myself for a week, at least she knows I'll be able to stay warm no matter what happens.

3. Bring an extra flashlight rather than extra batteries. If the flashlight breaks all the batteries in the world won't help.

4. When hanging your food to avoid feeding the black bears, bring at least 50 feet of lightweight nylon rope (parachute cord is excellent). Less rope makes it very difficult to properly hang food.

5. If you travel alone, as I sometimes do (and I'm not going to tell you not to travel alone since, if you are like me, you probably hear that from your family often enough), leave your itinerary with someone and don't deviate from the planned route. It's comforting for everyone (yourself included) to know that if you become disabled someone knows where you are and when you should return. If you break your ankle you know there is no need to panic—help will soon be on the way, and they know where to look for you— just sit tight and wait.

6. Buy the best hiking boots and backpack that you can afford. That 10-20 dollars you skimped on will seem like a paltry sum when you're 30 miles from civilization and are sweating up a pass with blisters or sore shoulders.

7. Carry a compass and know how to use it—even if you don't plan on leaving the trail.

8. Expect the worst possible weather and pack for it. The few extra ounces a rain poncho weighs could save the day for you.

9. If you're not opposed to wearing a watch (some people like to get away from everything when hiking—including the confinements of time) figure your own hiking speed. This way you'll have a good idea where you are when it's a long way between trail signs and obvious physical features of the terrain. This is most important when traveling cross-country or on trails with no signs. For example, my own formula when carrying a full backpack is 20 minutes per level trail mile (when I'm acclimated and in reasonably good physical condition). I add two minutes per 100 feet of elevation gain. So, if I'm looking for a side trail that should be two miles away, and my topo map shows a 400 foot climb in those two miles, I should reach it in about 48 minutes. This helps me immensely when planning where to camp, how long to fish, etc. Knowing my pace has helped me many times when I may have otherwise taken a wrong turn or missed a landmark.

10. Give yourself as much time as possible to acclimate. If you're coming from sea level to a 9,000 foot elevation trailhead, altitude sickness is just waiting to snare you. Try to drive up the night before and spend the night—it can make a huge difference in your hiking ability the next day. When gaining altitude on a hike drink lots of water—it is a great defense against altitude sickness.

Fly Tying Instructions For Sierra Bug

Hook: *Dry fly 14-22*
Thread: *Black*
Body: *Black antron*
Hackle: *Black palmered*
Wing: *White or orange bucktail*

This fly can be made more versatile by varying the wing. The wing can be tied upright or down over the body depending on what insect you feel you're most likely to find. I prefer a white wing for lakes and an orange wing for rivers. The orange doesn't get lost in the white water of a river, but it tends to be a little bright for the smooth surface of a lake. Either wing can be clipped off entirely if you encounter selective trout and good visibility. In addition to passing for terrestrial ants, beetles, mayflies, midges and caddisflies, the white-winged version matches the many flying ants found in the Sierra. The orange-winged fly makes an excellent impression of a ladybug. I carry Sierra Bugs in several sizes with both white and orange wings.

Bibliography

Books

Brooks, Charles, *Larger Trout for the Western Flyfisherman*. New York: Nick Lyons Books, 1983.

Brooks, Joe, *Trout Fishing*. New York: Harper and Row, 1972.

Hafele, Rick and Dave Hughes, *The Complete Book of Western Hatches*. Portland: Frank Amato Publications, 1982.

Hutchings, J. M., *In the Heart of the Sierra's*. Oakland: Pacific Press Publishing House, 1886.

Muir, John, *The Yosemite*. New York: The Century Company, Inc., 1912.

Schaffer, Jeffrey, *Yosemite National Park*. Berkeley: Wilderness Press, 1989.

Wolfe, Linnie Marsh, ed. *John of the Mountains—The Unpublished Journals of John Muir*. Boston: Houghton Mifflin Co., 1938.

Reports and Bulletins

Comprehensive Review of Trout Fishing Problems of Yosemite National Park. Yosemite Trout Investigations, 1952, O.L. Wallis.

High Lakes Survey 1977, Status of Fish Populations in 102 Planted Lakes. Stephen J. Botti, Dana L. Finney, Robert R. Smith, E.J. Koford.

Summer Fish Population Survey—Upper Merced River Watershed. 1992, Fred Bertetta, Jr.

Superintendent Reports to the U.S. Secretary of the Interior. 1892-1933, National Park Service.

Trout of California. 1969, California Department of Fish and Game.

Yosemite National Park Fish Stocking Record 1933-1979. National Park Service.

Yosemite Nature Notes. 1921-1961, Yosemite Natural History Association, National Park Service.